"SELLING IS NOT *JUST* TELLING"

Selling is easy if you know what and how to communicate

Written by someone who knows Sales and
Marketing TED TODD (PhD) Ex Owner of
Ted's Cameras, Melbourne Australia)

Selling and achieving better earnings and an easier and smoother way of life in the selling profession

In the Australian retail trade TED Todd (now ex) of Ted's CAMERAS is a bit of a legend. The cartooned face is recognized all over Australia. Ted migrated to Australia from Hungary in 1956. In 1970 he established the well-known and respected retail chain TED'S CAMERA STORE. Since the sale of that business, Ted has facilitated sales and marketing workshops and consultancy at the Australian Institute of Management and other venues, operated other businesses, and concurrently facilitated 'Human Relationships' courses for the past 33 years. In later years, Ted went back to tertiary studies, attaining a B.A and a Grad. Dip in Human Relationships Education, and now a PhD.

Ted Todd has written not only this book on sales/marketing/communications, but also two works of fiction "A Doubtful Inheritance" is about many things; the migrant experience, growing up, finding roots and losing them, money inherited and lost, a feelings and thought inherited and found, and a search for identity and happiness.

Also fiction is "Fifty Something Male looking for A woman..." a bunch of somewhat connected short stories about men over 50 after a broken marriage who are looking for a new intimate partner, love, romance, lust...The book considers how and what man and women may feel and think at that first meeting, why things do or do not work out, and who is doing what to whom... The stories are variously serious, funny, and touching, pathos is ever present as are the oddities of that first meeting between a man and a woman

Also, Ted calls his nonfiction book titled "The Software of the Personality" (copyright). As Ted puts it: 'a sort of self-help/philosophical and psychological meandering'... An unusual way of looking at and researching one's personality with a view to an improved way of life, thinking and emotions. The book is jargon free, aims at practical and usable ideas and ways of think and acting about one's life issues.

All book are available in paperback or Ebook from Amazon Kindle, Apple books, Google books etc and from better book stores

Copyright © 2018 Dr. Ted Todd

All rights reserved worldwide.

No part of the book may be copied or changed in any format, sold, or used in a way other than what is outlined in this book, under any circumstances, without the prior written permission of the publisher.

Publisher: BLUESTONE PUBLISHING, MELBOURNE AUSTRALIA

Author: Todd, Ted

Title: *Selling Is Not Just Telling*

Subjects: Selling.

Marketing.

Sales promotion. Interpersonal communication.

ISBN paperback: 9780648545408

ISBN Ebook: 9780648545415

CONTENTS

Introduction 1

Chapter 1: What is selling? 15

Chapter 2: Learning new skills 33

Chapter 3: Selling solutions – a sort of 'staircase' model 43

Chapter 4: The agreement summary of selling – a series of steps 65

Chapter 5: Add on selling is advanced selling and service ... 103

Chapter 6: The great, and small bunkums of selling 135

Chapter 7: Enhanced professional selling, marketing and promoting & high quality personal and business communications 149

Chapter 8: Exploring human behaviour, conduct and performance is exciting, but it can be confusing 175

Chapter 9: Body language and time management 185

Chapter 10: Creativity at work and at home 191

Chapter 11: Self-acceptance equals success? 205

Summary: Make more sales, stop selling. Find solutions and influence others. 209

INTRODUCTION

This book is aimed at both the new and the experienced professional salesperson. Also at those people who can (and will) see that the selling solutions/communication skills offered here are sensible and also facilitate great personal relating between any two or more people.

Selling[1] can be one of the most misunderstood professions, it is also the best and the worst paid employment. It is highly regarded by some people and viewed with much disdain by others. The selling profession has not always had a good reputation in spite of it being so widespread and absolutely vital to all of us. This is due to unprofessional salespeople with a 'real deal,' flashy fast talkers, or those non-caring in the real sense. These 'salesmen' are all seen by customers for what they really are: not good enough, or worse, petty crooks not to be trusted.

Selling, buying and doing business is likely the oldest and most important of professions. The exchange of goods, ideas and relationships is very much an integral part of the way the world operates and has brought about cultural exchange, understanding and interaction and a sense of inter-dependence between the peoples of the earth.

To communicate well is to get and give what you want, and it is not always easy. We are not born into it, we can learn to do better at work, at home and within ourselves.

SELLING IS NOT *JUST* TELLING

> The word 'selling' has acquired a kind of cheap connotation. I shall use the word in this book for simplicity, but what this book aims to achieve is to help people achieve better results at work and at home!

When it comes to making a living, or having an intimate relationship with another, we can say that one way or another everyone is involved in some sort 'selling' and/or 'buying.' In truth, when it comes to relating to other people, in the course of just living our lives, we may say that we are often 'peddling' something in order to get what we want or need, and conversely we are being 'sold', even if it is no more than agreeing to going to the restaurant your partner prefers to eat in.

Selling can be anything from the banal to the complex professional stuff. Most of the time, in a personal sense, we are not even aware that we are selling!

AND RIGHT HERE IS THE DIFFERENCE BETWEEN A PRO AND AN AMATEUR

A huge difference folks, between the people who 'sell' on purpose and those who just live as it were, by undirected accidents. More about this later, but this so called accidental living happens to the great majority of people in all professions - and in all their personal relating. As promised, in this work we are tackling selling in a commercial sense, at all levels – retail, wholesale, marketing broadly and so on. Still, the main aim and thrust of this book can be described as being more for retail selling. Good thinkers will, however, find it easy to convert from retail ideas to a greater or slower selling cycle.

A career salesperson, a professional, is one who is always aware of what is going on. In personal life too, it is better to know how to

INTRODUCTION

get more of what we want and need. No, it is not manipulation, as you will see in a later chapter.

> **We are all 'sales' people looking for 'solutions'
> results, success, happiness or whatever...
> even when we are 'buying' something**

> We are all involved in selling and buying. Not only professional salespeople sell, but also doctors, politicians, parents, children and even people wanting to establish, or keep and improve their personal relationships. Some people may object that some of the more personal pursuits like establishing relationships are not 'selling' as such. But real selling, as far as I am concerned, is nothing more or less than excellent communication that brings people together.

There is nothing better than being a professional salesperson, providing that you are **suited** to it, and assuming you have a good grasp of what 'solution' selling and thus influencing others is really about.. Fortunately, you don't need to be an absolute champion, all you need to be is just that tiny bit better than the competition. You do not need to become the best. You just need to be a smidgen ahead, a tiny bit more professional that is all, and huge sales and personal rewards will follow.

Some people can become very good at professionally selling products and services, others at selling or communicating ideas. Not everyone has exactly the right personality to be good at selling products. Everyone can improve their ability to be better at selling and at one of the most amazing aspects of life: successfully communicating with other people.

WHO AND WHAT IS THE 'CUSTOMER'? EVERYONE, YOURSELF INCLUDED IS A 'CUSTOMER'

Everyone you sell to or negotiate with is a customer. Let us add one more 'customer' to the list, the most important one, the one who is always buying or selling something – YOU. Who else do you deal with, sell to or buy from 24 hours a day? You sell yourself ideas, decisions and actions. You talk yourself into and out of things all day, even in your sleep sometimes. This is an important idea to be aware of since there is no one who does not 'sell' themselves some good, or some less worthy, at times even silly ideas.

No one should try to manipulate others. Yet we all try doing so to a degree time and again and in spite of the fact that we know that manipulative behavior often fails. When you know how to 'sell' properly you are not manipulating but exchanging ideas and satisfying both the seller and the buyer. That is the big difference.

> Although this book is mainly concerned with those of us who are pursuing selling as a profession not as a 'get rich quick' scheme, or as a temporary thing until we find something better, this book is also aimed at everyone: we are all buying and selling things throughout our lives.
>
> **We are all entitled to influence each other in a productive and positive sense in order to find better solutions that deliver what each of us wants and needs.**

∼

To achieve anything at all, you need to know how to best reach out for it. Focused communication is clearly the way; and though

INTRODUCTION

everyone readily agrees to this, communications is still a rarely practiced and very misunderstood skill. **Selling success is nothing but good communication skills used appropriately in a focused manner,** as opposed to manipulative behaviour. Manipulate others in that bad sense of the word and you are manipulating yourself and vice versa. Be good at what you do or you will waste of your life, one day wondering what has happened to your dreams and relationships.

What do I know about selling and communicating?

I suggest that thinking about selling solutions or benefits as **focused communication** skills will change the way you sell, buy and relate to others. This leads to less stress and more rational and fun living.

This book has come from 40 years of experience of selling products and ideas in the retail and industrial settings. Since the sale of my business I have worked as a consultant and trainer-facilitator in communications, selling, and in human relationships workshops at the Australian Institute of Management, the ACF, Oxfam and at various other places.

Many years ago when I was a well-known retailer (Ted's Camera Stores, Genius photo and Video, Health Food Times, etc.) I constantly tried to find new ways of explaining to my sales staff that selling needs to be done in a professional way. How was I going to 'sell' the idea of good selling and focused communications to salespeople?

Selling, I explained to my staff, is not something we do by accident as the customer walks into the store:

'SELLING IS NOT JUST TELLING.'

'SELLING IS NOT JUST TELLING' is the best one line idea I have ever had. Yet to this day, (perhaps it is worse than ever) many people employed in selling and marketing, still do just that: they do telling, talking, and rave on...but they are not selling! Like in any profession, there are proper ways, techniques and rules to get the best results and to find the 'right solutions.'

Contrary to what's been the accepted norm, I don't believe you can 'leave your problems at home' so easily. What you can do is learn to control and even use them in some sales situations.

INTRODUCTION

In selling, you meet new people all the time and you deal with new products, technology and interesting and exciting changes in the market place. The challenge is great and those who rise to it do very well; top salespeople are some of the best-paid people on earth. What a wonderful profession selling can be! It is an amazing thing to sell products or ideas. Within a few minutes of meeting a customer, you are asking, usually a total stranger, to trust and believe you and to spend money with you. In that brief time you need to establish a long- lasting customer relationship. (Yes, even if you will never see them again.)

ALL THESE QUESTIONS ARE STUPID, UNNCESSARY AND A WASTE OF TIME

The concepts and ideas that I will suggest in this book may surprise and challenge you. Many people have some set, and usually not very productive or clear ideas on selling. I hope to change that.

The first part of this book deals with focused communications aimed at practical selling. In this section you'll tackle the selling steps and techniques from start to finish.

The second part of the book deals with the deeper and subtler issues and techniques of advanced selling and more. You will be asked to wrestle with some new ideas; issues of personality, which are very relevant to how you operate in business and/or in your private life. It is a slightly psychological look, but don't worry, it is a practical and jargon-free way to understand better why or how you operate as you do.

The two sections overlap and interact; each section explains issues about the other section more fully. I recommend that first you read the whole book as it is laid out. That done, your selling will improve and become more fun, less stressed. Then I suggest a second read of the whole thing. It is imperative that you learn the Selling Steps by heart. You will find ideas in the second part that need personal exploration and work in a deeper way.

SELLING IS A COOPERATIVE FOCUSED COMMUNICATION BETWEEN YOU AND THE CUSTOMER

I've never liked saying 'selling technique' because it sounds like something you do to others, a scheme that you throw out there and bingo, you get a result. Not so. I am also very aware that there are many books and workshops out there on selling that seem convincing, (and some have good ideas), but few readers have

INTRODUCTION

become great sellers merely reading them. You don't become an Olympic swimmer by reading a book about swimming techniques. Selling is not something you can just learn the words to; and it's certainly not a matter of something you *do* to others. And oh man or woman, there are so many salespeople who do just that, and they bore customers and partners and are usually bored to hell themselves. Surprising that they are badly paid?

> **Selling is a solution** to a want or need. It is what you do **WITH** the customer; a cooperative effort. Yet you, as the salesperson, have a great deal of **influence** on the outcome of any sales situation.

The skills outlined in this book are the rules of focused communication methods aimed at arriving at an outcome, an agreement, A SALE – SOLUTION, that is a jointly good deal for the customer; whether you are selling a camera, a building, a political idea... looking for a date...or making a deal with your wife/husband/partner. Such skills are not manipulation, or pushy behavior, far from it. I repeat that such skills are focused communications used for mutual benefit.

I hasten to add that you should not tell something to anyone who truly does not wish to buy your product. How do you know who might want to buy? How do you know who you might wish to relate to? Both questions will be clearly answered later. Knowing who does or does not wish to buy is emphatically a skill you can learn to employ...And it will stop you wasting some of your efforts, emotions, energy and expertise.

All my ideas owe something to the many people who taught me about selling, communications, philosophy, psychology and other areas of human behaviour. A few of these people were professionals on the subject of selling, but most of my real teachers were, and are, the customers and other salespeople I deal with.

Selling is properly focused communication that aims to influence, educate and inform a potential buyer

Our focus here is very much on 'selling' but I reiterate that good selling must always lead to and be a part of good living. Great communicators are, or can be, brilliant salespeople. Truly great salespeople are excellent communicators. Good communicators live better lives, have more successful relationships and greater appreciation of other people and the world they live in. You can be a great communicator only if you have what it takes (and most people do to various degrees), and if you know what you are doing; and doing it right becomes not your second, but your first effort.

This book looks at aspects not usually found in other books on selling.

One aspect of what we explore is about how your **personality** influences what you do or leave undone in selling and life situations. This is a bigger issue than many care to believe. Each of us is a complex communication pattern taking part in the greater relating that is living. What this means is that we must look at our own makeup, and that of others as 'personalities acting and doing' in the world. We must consider our motivations and actions as sellers and the customers' impulses as buyers, always keeping in mind that we are all people with thoughts and feelings, desires, needs, goals and aims.

We, salespeople, (and who is not?) have or can have a lot of influence on the decision making process of customers. I said that everyone is a customer; your partner, the kids, and real customers. To know how to exercise your power of influence is another thing you were not born with, but it is one you can learn.

INTRODUCTION

Your personality, behaviour, actions and abilities are not set in stone. It just (sometimes) seems that way.

Now read this carefully please

You may have, and I suggest you do have abilities and talents that you have not yet discovered. Your personality, as it applies to selling, can be better used. This is a big statement and perhaps a puzzling one. I will offer practical ways of **accessing** those parts of yourself that will work better for you. We'll look at how all this operates for you and your 'customers' at work and at home. Doing this sort of work is easy and interesting and even, fun.

YOUR PROCESS OF LEARNING SKILLS

Most people pay scant attention to the importance of the process they use for learning new skills. Given you are reading this book you are trying to learn how to improve your sales and likely, this is not the first time you have read a self help book. You may have read or heard a fair bit of material on selling, already. So, how much of it stuck in your mind to be of real help? Usually, and for most of us, very little and not for long. Then, we slip back into the tired old selling ways. BORING!

To learn well and to put new learning into lasting practice, you need to know your individual **best learning process**. We need to understand that the process of learning includes that of unlearning useless, habitual, old stuff. First, we need to know what and how we think/feel when we are learning. So, let's now look at how and what we do or have learned, and what stops us from learning and applying the new skills we want.

How come it's so hard to integrate newly learned material even if we actually like the new things we have learned? Earlier I mentioned **'your particular learning process,'** in addition to the general way most of us learn. This is where we start to look at the concept of how each of us have particular traits and abilities that make up our personality.

Your unique personality makes a difference to your actions and to the way you relate to the world; to the way you sell. Your personality is not set in stone; change is possible. My view is that there are three major factors involved in successful learning in order to bring about real and lasting change. As it happens, such 'features' are the very same ones that I shall use when we discuss hands-on selling:

<u>Learning and keeping great new skills needs a consideration of</u>

1. Your personality traits
2. Your ability to understand the new material
3. Your current life and selling situation

We will look at this in more detail for both the learning procedure and the selling process shortly.

SO, WHAT DO I ACTUALLY OFFER IN THIS BOOK?

The following ideas will help you to acquire and keep new skills and abilities. They will help you to achieve what you aim for. You will find good, practical and sane, rather than insane torturous selling techniques, and will also get to know yourself better than you did before. That means improved relationships at home and at work, as well as better sales and earnings.

INTRODUCTION

The various ideas I shall propose are not only reasonable, sensible and successful. I know from personal experience that what I suggest here can be learned and put into action by nearly anyone. And quickly. By the end of the book, if you understand and practice what I have offered, you will be a better communicator in both your business and private life. And let me assure you it is not that difficult to be more successful.

Again I emphasize this: the self-explorative nature of these ideas will bring more than just dollars into your life. This kind of learning and exploration of ideas are multi-pronged and propose:

- New ways to understand the skills you need for sales/marketing and for personal communications.

- Your ideas and understanding of the selling profession, and your part in it will change and be more relaxed.

- Personal adaptation of a set of selling procedures and self- explorative ideas that suit YOU, will make selling easier and far more successful.

'Personal adaptation' did I say? This is part of what is different in my way of selling/relating. You will be adopting and adapting to a particular set of selling/communicating skills that are easiest and best for you. Exactly how will depend on your particular personality. This major issue will need serious consideration. And I will offer such later. Everyone knows and agrees that nothing works equally well for everyone. Some will work for Joe but not for Jill or for Harry. Yet little if any attention is paid to the issue that you must *adapt* techniques to yourself, dropping some altogether, using some more - or less, but always using the basis. Always and only in honest ways, need I say.

SELLING IS NOT *JUST* TELLING

One other point to keep in mind before we move on is that some seemingly good skills are misunderstood, and misused in certain situations by many sellers. The big thing to understand is that everyone can improve his or her communications and thus aspects of selling.

CHAPTER 1

WHAT IS SELLING?

SELLING IS PROFESSIONALLY HELPING OTHERS GET WHAT THEY WANT OR NEED; FINDING SOLUTIONS!

What's wrong with the selling profession? Possibly, there has been more written on the selling/marketing aspects of doing business than on anything else. Unfortunately,

I found a lot of it was wasted reading and time spent in rooms, with other bored to death salespeople. Let's face it, most of what salespeople have been told to do has never worked well for most of us if at all. Lots of it has been also misunderstood, and so misused the selling procedures.

Unsurprisingly, those of us who work in sales have learned most of the craft by watching others in the sales environment. From an early age we have seen and experienced sales staff and customer service in shops. These points of contact have given us an idea – usually a bad one that resulted in many of us copying a great deal of bad behavior, and so and bad selling skills without even knowing we have done so.

Many mistakes have been made in suggestions and in judgments about what a salesperson is capable of, or should be capable of. Many more mistakes are made about what the customer really wants or needs. One sad reason for all these errors is that selling in our society is still based on get-rich quick schemes and on mistaken assumptions that the 'customer' can be controlled. Perhaps some customers can be manipulated, but this is not only undesirable, it really does not work, particularly if we want to sustain a long-term advantage over our competitors. When selling is manipulative the customer and salesperson are inclined to be wary of each other rather than figure out exactly what will seal the deal to their mutual satisfaction.

Another vitally important point, as already mentioned, is that some very good sales ideas for some reason do not work for lots of salespeople. Most books and courses on selling would have us believe that it is easy to sell providing we follow exactly what is being offered. Well, yes and definitely no.

If all we have to do is to read the latest and greatest version of some of the many often torturous new schemes, then why aren't we all great salespeople who are making lots of money? I believe I have the right answer to that.

Many offerings tell us that we need to learn good communication skills. Fair enough, I also say that. But then we are also told a lot of rather silly stuff. We are told to view the world positively each morning, never feel rejected, and walk on hot coals to prove that we can do anything etc. There is a lot of nonsense amongst the pearls of wisdom. I certainly do not recommend either get-rich-quick schemes or walking on hot coals. And no friends, you can't be anything you want, you cannot do anything you wish…as most of us have already found out.

When I was a new young salesman I was told to 'fake it till you make it.' This too was one of the silliest one-liners ever to come into common usage. It is a miserable idea that will simply not work, not in anything, let alone selling, and not for long at any rate.

Something is wrong with all the self-help books and courses.

I mean this not only with regard to books and courses on selling, but also around teachings about painting, or Buddhism or playing footy. After all, just by reading a book or attending a workshop or two we do not rise to great heights in any endeavour. Invariably the reader-student is blamed either overtly or covertly. The assumption is that if the student did it exactly the way the teachings suggest, they would get there. Yet, most of us never get anywhere near 'there.'

'It's time', as Gough Whitlam famously said many years ago, 'time for a change.' Surely it is not just the student's fault that they do not become an immediate and huge success simply by reading the books or doing the odd course. The teaching, ideas and systems must also be somewhat at fault.

**Perhaps insufficient attention is paid
to the situations of real life?**

Ask any salesperson about the difference between the idealism books offer about selling and the real world and you will get an earful. If you have ever sold anything, or tried to convince others about something, you will know that customers rarely follow the script. (Perhaps they should be made to read the books, huh?) Unfortunately, most salespeople, i.e. students of the art of selling, do not become what is promised; they do not rise to the heady levels of success the examples in books tell us about. I believe the missing link is to ADAPT good material to YOURSELF. Meaning, that you simply must find and use that part of your personality that works best for the task at hand when <u>adopting and adapting</u> the techniques of selling and communication. [1]

~

Have you picked up on my constant coupling of selling and communications yet? I hope so for the two are really only ONE, but focused on a particular issue. My effort around selling an idea to my wife is one, and selling a camera to a customer is another, a very different focus and yet the underlying basic skills are very similar. More on this later for I can just hear people in personal relationships who do not want to be 'sold' to. But stay with me on this one for a while and consider how each of us already do, in fact, sell to our wives or husbands, children, friends and so on.

Most people like the idea of having a blueprint about selling or about living well. But hey, there is no actual foolproof blueprint about how to sell or about how to live best. What we can do is draw from some practical guidelines, add our own past experience and then adapt it all to our particular working situation and, of course, personality. From there on, it's about creatively innovating and improving from that basis.

Ask most people who have run a business, a committee, or a football club, or a home, and they will tell you that when it comes to getting things done, well it is a good idea to pick 'horses for courses.' They usually also add that if you want to be sure of getting things done correctly you often have to do it yourself. Familiar? All I'm suggesting is that things do not work out well if you pick the wrong horse for the course, even if you are the horse!

---

[1] Adopting is a bit like adopting a child. Adapting is altering what there is to work best in a situation

WHAT IS SELLING?

Now I will spell it out even more: you need to find your own best *features, abilities and personality traits* that work best in selling and communicating. How do you know which 'parts' of you help or hinder your selling? What do you know of the abilities you have or could activate but have not yet done so? Are you truly familiar with what you have/are? What sort of inner/outer attitude will work for you when selling? These are worthy questions to get a grip on.

How you communicate is always directed by the type of person you are. Your particular communication style may or may not be suitable for selling just as it is, but it can be changed, often quickly and easily, though sometimes only with an extra effort (and sometimes not at all). There is no sure-fire way, no instruction book, I said, and yet there are basic structures, many of them very good. Adopt and adapt them

To know yourself takes some work and effort. Many of us, myself included, fell into the sales profession by accident. I stayed there because I liked it. Many others stay for reasons which are not good. If you are in sales, service or marketing not by accident, how do you know you've picked the right profession? Are you selling the sorts of products that are best suited to you? My proposal is repeatedly to say that you need to find the 'right horse' within your own personality, the one that can do selling-communicating in the best possible way.

Consider the following 3 points throughout this book:

- Selling is not just 'telling'
- Selling should be a well-motivated and sharply focused communication.

SELLING IS NOT *JUST* TELLING

- Selling and communicating above average means adapting new learning to yours personality and abilities.

Let's have a closer look at these points and debunk some nonsense about selling. Can anything be 'sold' to anyone? I do not think so. Some sales managers might object when I say that it is at the very least debatable that people can actually be 'sold' things. People will buy things if they need or want them. It is the job of the marketing and promotional people to inform customers about new products and to create the desire in customers to buy products. Once a product is marketed, personal selling comes into the picture. This is where great sales skills really matter, as there are many businesses selling very similar or exactly the same products.[2]

You cannot and should not try to 'sell' things to someone who does not want them. For example, there is no way anyone can sell me a gun or a can of smoked oysters (yuck!) But perhaps at another time, if I have a need for a steam train or a can of smoked oysters, my 'absolutely not' may change. At that time a salesperson will be able to sell me either this or that particular product, providing I get good information and assurance from the salesperson.

This is the point when the professionalism of the salesperson becomes the most important link between buyers and manufacturers of products. It is at this point we can truly say that one person can, and another cannot sell the very same item. The point I want to emphasize is that if a product is wanted or needed and your sales presentation is good then customers are likely to buy from you. Yet so many times they don't buy! It is up to you, the seller, to convince the buyer that the product, the service offered and the deal is a good one. And it is up to you to know

---

[2] In another special chapter I shall discuss the end of an era, the end of selling the product first. Now we need to sell our business first, or the overseas Internet online sellers will take away our business; retail and manufacturing.

WHAT IS SELLING?

why you lost the sale, as far as that is possible, and it is possible to know this most of the time.

SELLING IS NOT JUST TELLING; INFLUENCING PEOPLE IS NOT ALL TALK!

Yet, talking and 'telling' is what most salespeople do, and overdo, when they think that they are selling. All sorts of salespeople, not only retailers, talk too much. Most salespeople talk far more than their customers, and more than they need to. Worse still, salespeople talk about lots things the customer does not want or need to hear. To sell, it is imperative that the customer does more talking, at least in the early stage.

Here is a caution about some of the telling we should not do:

Selling is not a discussion about footy, their state of health or other nonsense issues. The customer did not come to see you about, nor does s/he wants to know or believe that you have just sold one of these gadgets to your grandpa, or that you sold twelve in a week, etc. etc. Then again, most of the 'telling' sellers tend to just list features or offer frivolous words about how good or popular the B123 computers are.

Salespeople should not actively lie, nor say what they think the customer might wish to hear. Then again, if you think the hot pink dress does not suit your customer, perhaps you need not say so; it may just be your opinion. 'Silence is golden' my wise grandma used to tell me. Sometimes it is better not to say anything.

When a customer is looking for a video camera it might be better not to mention a $3000 camera if you know that a $1500 camera will do the job. The customer does want to hear your opinion about various products but probably not about the need to spend twice as much as they wish to spend. Then again the decision as to whether the customer spends $1500 or $3000 is up to the customer. The sales person needs to make a decision on this point and perhaps offer, inform and explain why a dearer model might be more satisfactory to this customer. Telling instead of selling is just words, often without aim or focus and certainly not influencing the buyers. No wonder so many sales staff are bored beyond belief. In any case imagine that the customer does not like what you say. And they won't like anything you say unless you have made your approach correctly. That is, unless what you say is focused on the **worries and issues the customer has**. That, dear salesperson reading this book, is the big and salient question! Finding out what the customer's concerns and interests are before launching into any selling as such. So, you must stop 'telling' and learn to listen. Listening is a big part of selling and the only way to go when selling a product to customers or selling yourself to whomever.

CUSTOMERS ARE DIFFERENT EVERY TIME

A sixty-year-old male customer, a twenty-one year old young lady and a middle-aged executive in his impeccable Gucci suit are looking for a new video camera. All three appear to be after the same product. They all say they want something fully automatic, relatively easy and simple to use. They might even nominate a recently advertised brand and model. This sounds easy to handle so far. Like most politicians do in our times I'd have to lose the unlosable election in order to not win the sale. Still, I will not win the sale if I do not look for some of the potential emotions, needs and aims that are behind the motivation to buy.

As it turns out, the sixty year old has just had his first grandchild. The young lady has just started a college course in cinema studies and the Gucci suit is going overseas to suss out the forthcoming Parisian fashion designs. 'So what?' I have heard people during workshops ask me. 'So what?' Why do we need to know what they

WHAT IS SELLING?

want to do with the product? Sounds like a good question but it is a bad question that should be discarded. Salespeople simply must show interest in what the goods will be used for, and if they listen well to the customer much will be revealed during the client's answer. Plus, no customer will fail to be impressed with your enquiry and interest, if it is well done. It is the first step to building the selling relationship.

It is necessary for the salesperson to know about the motivations of these three customers since they are obviously driven by different needs. To learn these things from the customer the seller needs to ask questions and listen very carefully. Clearly, without knowing what is going on in the mind of each customer, no amount of 'telling' will assist the sale. But once you know something about the customer's needs you can actively engage customer and brand/model with the outcomes the client seeks.

Customer-focused selling and good communication is the same thing.

Selling rather than just telling, is what being customer-focused means. Everyone agrees about customer focused selling but few practice it properly. What does it mean? If we are not talking with the customer from their point of view then we will miss the mark and lose the sale. When you are customer-focused, taking the needs and wishes of the buyer into serious and proper consideration, things will work to the satisfaction of the customer; a sale and a return client is made. Remember these 3 points:

- Selling that is not customer-focused is 'telling' not selling.

- Business can only be successful and honourable if it is done with care and concern for the customer and for their point of view.

SELLING IS NOT *JUST* TELLING

- Customers want what money on its own cannot buy: satisfaction.

- The seller who is not properly listening and responding to the customer is like the Internet, showing and telling, not selling. That's why the Internet will never replace a truly skilled communicator salesperson.

> Every (so-called) difficult buyer who has not purchased a product or a service from you will buy somewhere else.

Good salespeople earn the sale by providing customer focused service. This means salespeople need to develop:

- Confidence. Not the pretend type, but real confidence that comes from knowing your products and by using professional sales skills as a focused piece of communication everytime.

- The ability to use effective communication styles with each individual customer and situation. This can only happen if knowledge of communication styles is an 'automatic' competence or skill.

- Understanding of themselves, their features and abilities, preferences, values and motivations. Understanding of other people's and their own personality types and styles.

- The ability to create a positive, safe, 'fun' buying experience, which brings customers back.

- Understanding and commitment to the aims and goals of their company. These should be always in the forefront of a salesperson's mind. You and the people you work with are all wearing the same Guernsey and cooperating as a team.

(I have made references to several issues in the above points that we have not yet discussed, but we will cover them later as they are rather important).

Customer-focused selling starts with the actuality that people may be similar and yet very different.

Most training about selling suggests that there is a tried and true recipe for selling that works with everyone in all situations. Think about it. Is it possible to sell in exactly the same way to everyone and anyone? Could the same rules and techniques be applied in the same way to influence anyone and everyone? How could the same techniques be applied to complex and simple products, to cheap or expensive products, or for goods which are new tech or old, or to items which are needed like a fridge, compared with luxury items like a video camera?

The sales performance, the communication steps taken may be similar every time, but the customers are not. You need to adapt the techniques to each customer.

To assume that all customers are alike is not just silly, but arrogant. Customers are as individual as salespeople. My suggestions are aimed to allow for the differences of personalities and products and to use these differences in an ethical and profitable way.

You might be really good at some aspects of selling and less so at others. You are who you are, and how you are, for now. Let's see if you can learn to use the best bits of yourself to your advantage and improve or develop your abilities as you go. Customers notice your intentions, product knowledge and how you really feel when selling. Customers perceive how much of a professional you really are, often without realizing it. If they don't buy, it's because they don't feel right about buying the product from you right now. You have not influenced them!

> If your customer, wife, child or mate is uncertain about what you are 'selling' or offering, if they cannot see a *solution* they can recognize and like, it is a NO sale. Perhaps because you have not unearthed what would assure them that what you are offering is a solution for them.

There are certainly times when the client is not ready to buy today. That is ok because so as long as you have done a professional job of the presentation, the customer will come back. You know this is true because it often happens but, the big but is, not with every customer. 'Why not?' is the big question, but suffice it to say that if you improve your total presentation, more clients will come back.

SUCCESSFUL PEOPLE MUST BE SUCCESSFUL AT WORK AND AT HOME

We spend a lot of our lives at work. It involves us socially and it incorporates our private lives and families as well. Work either supplies us with meaning and satisfaction or it is drudgery, boredom, disappointment and doesn't pay well. Our working lives are long, but no one would disagree that it is not just dollars we work for. Yet many people hate their jobs or barely put up with them. Many people ruin their relationships at home by doing too much work, or too little. Most people seem to settle for a 'get away with it' scenario, the 'I go to work to get paid' attitude. This state of affairs is not as good as you can get. You can do far, far better than this. I hope to be of help in showing you how to improve your selling skills and at the same time improve your private life because there are close connections between the two.

We have mentioned the **adapting of new skills**. Learning new ideas needs you to effect three important adaptations:

- Adapting the ideas to yourself, to the kind of person you actually are.

- Adapting your particular style of selling to match the situation you are in.

- Adapting your communication style to suit each individual customer.

These three points make all the difference when you are trying to improve your selling skills and/or your private life. The three-way adaptation may often be the missing link. No one can learn what I or anyone else offers and use that knowledge, without adapting the learning to his or her particular features and abilities, personality and life situation.

> Non-achievers always have a reason and a story as to what went wrong and what they ought to be doing next. While they are doing that, talking about their bad luck or the rotten boss, they don't notice that they are talking about the 'plan' endlessly. Meanwhile, successful people are out there actually getting the job done.

GOAL SETTING – 'JUST DO IT' (NIKE)

When the Nike people came up with the famous one liner – "Just Do It" – it was an instant success as a marketing campaign. But we all know that saying 'Just Do It' is easy. It gives one a feeling of almost arrogance, gives one a lift – just get out there and do it. It is easy to say and easy to understand. Is it easy to do? Sure, if and when it is easy. Unfortunately, for most of us the doing is usually a bit harder than the famous line suggests. In truth, it is nearly impossible to 'Just Do It' when it comes to real change and real improvement in selling, unless you have the right level of competence to do it. It is not very hard to gain enough know-how to get it right, but it does take some perseverance.

What do we need to 'just do it' to set a sensible achievable goal?

- Self-knowledge. This includes being familiar with how you operate in your life and accepting the way the world is for you right now. To move on and improve your life you need the next idea.

WHAT IS SELLING?

- You need to have the skills required to achieve what you want. Set attainable goals. Aim high, but aim reasonably. DO NOT set yourself up to fail.

- Learn from the past rather than dwell on it. Accept responsibility for your actions in the world by doing as well as you can for yourself and for others.

- You can change your life and aim high, but you may need to work at it with purpose and intention; not by accident, not without a plan, not acting like a drifting leaf.

The famous German author, Goethe, said words to the effect that enthusiasm and dreams of better things are great so long as a person does not let himself be carried away. Living in the real world, using what you have, doing what you can to improve your situation means taking action, making a real sustained effort, not just wishing and dreaming.

Dreaming a bigger dream and being enthusiastic is good and necessary and will carry more conviction if you know how to proceed. On the other hand, it is easy to cross the thin line into what is not yet (or may ever be) possible for you. The goal setting ideas of the 70's and 80's seemed very good to most of us but created a lot of heartbreak. Eventually, most people realized that they could not just decide to have, or to be anything at all.

Note that you cannot 'do' a goal. If you set a goal you need to ask:

'What do I need to do to realize this goal?' Then, look at whether you have what it takes, what you need to learn, and what are the associated risks. Imagine you are a salesperson and you have decided to set the goal to be the proud owner of a new Porsche by December. The questions are obvious. What do you need to earn between now and then? How will you do that? Is it possible

to do so? It might be a good question to ask whether this is a good goal in the long run. Is it possible to work hard enough to earn the dollars needed? Is it worth the effort?

Some things are easy to do and some are very hard.

This would be an empty truism but sometimes we get stuck in what we have and what we know about ourselves. There were many things that twenty years ago I found hard to do, a lot of which have now become easier. For example, I was a lousy student in school back then, but now I enjoy studying at the highest university level and I am getting better at it. In fact, I have PhD now and I am called Dr. Todd. It is not the title that matters, but what doors my education opens.

Other things that used to be easy have become harder, like running the marathon or starting a new profession or just improving what I do with my writing. When you decide to choose a goal, ask yourself whether you have a real interest and desire to put in the effort needed.

Thinking about all this may even help to cut some things out of your life, giving you more time, space and energy for those things that you really want to achieve. Sometimes it is not a bad 'goal' to give up some things.

So, choose carefully what you set out to achieve. Put simply, I really would like to become a jazz singer, but I haven't the voice for it, and that won't change now, no matter how hard or long I work at it. So for me, jazz singing as a goal is out. You might like to be a university professor, but studying has never appealed to you. You'd like to sell real estate but that needs a lot of patience and various other quirks of personality. I want to be a writer, but I am short on patience, hate typing, and my grammar is not so good.

WHAT IS SELLING?

To try to be what we cannot is not bad, it is just sad, and a waste of time. One thing's for sure in order to achieve what you want you will need to learn new skills.

Try this exercise. Don't think too hard, just be spontaneous for now.

1. On a blank sheet of paper draw three columns.

2. In the first column, write down what you find easy about your job.

3. In the third column write down what you find hard to do.

4. In the middle column write actions you find in between easy and hard.

5. Take another sheet of paper and draw three columns.

6. In the first column, list all the things you are good at.

7. In the middle column list down the ones that you are between good and bad at.

8. In the last column, list what you think you are bad at.

9. Overlap the two sheets and compare the job actions that you are good at, bad at or in between with the job actions that you found easy, hard and in-between.

You will find that what you are good at you usually find easy to do, what you find difficult or you are not so good at, and the things in between depend on various other factors.

The next question to ask yourself as part of this exercise is this: Is what you call easy, really easy and is what you call hard, really hard? Be realistic about it. What do I mean when I say 'really' easy or hard? Stop and consider whether you feel that doing something is easy or whether you just think it 'should' be easy, while in fact, it sends hot flushes into your brain and tummy. Don't fool yourself. The job skills in between easy and hard are usually those things that are relatively workable and can be tuned up to the 'easy' column fairly readily. The really hard stuff can also be improved though it takes more work and perseverance.

Make the most of your good points. There will be plenty of bad ones left.

If you think you are not good enough at everything about selling, then consider doing everything you are good at even better!

∼

We are now ready to move further into the details of our main points. You may have noticed that I have repeated some things up to this point. That is part of how we learn. Some people may wonder why I bothered with this next chapter on how we learn things. Why not go straight into the 'how to do it' steps? I have already said that a particular style of sales training, getting people to mug in the selling techniques have not worked all that well.

I shall now try to encourage you to consider that each of us needs to know and to formulate our very own 'learning process.'

CHAPTER 2

LEARNING NEW SKILLS

WHY NEW SKILLS ARE OFTEN QUICKLY LOST AND HOW TO KEEP THEM

Let's say that you have recently learned some fine new skills, but after a few weeks the new knowledge has faded away. It is forgotten or barely used. Why does this happen even when you agreed that the new ideas seemed good and were likely to be helpful? One reason is that the new knowledge you gained was not taken to the vital *automatic competence* stage. Another possible reason is that it was not fully adapted to yourself and to your situation. Your skill range includes a great deal of what is not always obvious. You may not be aware of the bad skills you use day by day, believing that they work. These are 'anti-skills' so to speak, and thus we often 'sell' in such ways, ways that are unlikely to succeed. Bad habits learned when you first try tennis or golf are easy to pick up and hard to give up. It is just the same with any other skill or technique. You cannot avoid picking up the bad with the good skills. Fortunately, when you get good techniques going and if they are set in you as *automatic competence*, consistently better results will follow. Good practices actually help to get rid of or squeeze out the bad stuff. Let's look at what you need to be aware of in order to really learn a new skill. The emphasis is on 'really' learning and that implies correct understanding, which in turn results in real learning. Shallow knowledge does not help your cause because it results in misunderstanding and misuse and when that happens, you quickly forget the ideas.

WHAT YOU NEED TO DO TO LEARN ANYTHING AT ALL

To start learning, you need to be open to the input of new information or material. Obvious, yes but there is a certain challenge in letting in new material. Your mind wants to relate and make sense of incoming information by comparing it to what it already knows. That is necessary and helpful, but it can also stop the understanding of new information and thus potentially block learning. Your mind usually wants to say, 'I know that already' and perhaps you do, but often it is the old 'as if' you know rather than real knowhow.

Repetitive learning.

We know that we learn by repetition, but it is not as simple as it seems. We do not necessarily learn anything new just by repetition. We also learn bad habits by repetition.

When we are consistently repeating actions to produce a certain result, we need to look at how each action taken has influenced that result. In other words, look at what worked well *and* what didn't work so well. People, institutions and companies usually look at what went wrong, but pay little or no attention to what went RIGHT! We need to evaluate what happened and understand how our actions have influenced the results.

LEARNING NEW SKILLS

Remember how you learned to ride a bike. You didn't just get on the bike and fall off and repeat getting on and falling off. Something else needed to happen in order for you to learn to ride. After you got up from each fall you had to think about what happened or someone had to tell you what you did wrong – you leaned too far to the right, or whatever. This is the evaluation stage of your action and result. If your evaluation tells you that leaning too far to the right makes you fall, then you know what you need to do to improve.

> The two-way evaluation is a must: what was good and what was bad tells you that the actions you have taken may have resulted in both positive and negative outcomes. For example, you may have leaned too far but applied the brakes at the right time. Perhaps you keep the good idea of braking at the right time, but make an effort to lean less to avoid falling.

Every time you learn and keep a new skill, whether it is good or bad, you have done it this way:

- You understood what you were meant to do. Then you put it into action. You noted and stored the experience irrespective of whether the results were perfect or not so good.

You do not learn by repetition of actions alone, you learn by repeating the evaluation process and changing your actions to get the desired results.

The above is, in a simplified way, how the learning process works. Most of the time you are not aware of this process, it seems to come naturally. But imagine falling off a bike and taking absolutely no notice of what happened. You'd keep falling off and never learn to ride. There are always these three steps in the learning process:

1. Understanding what to do
2. Taking action
3. Evaluating the results and doing it again.

Applying these three steps consciously will improve your results no matter what you are learning.

Learning better selling/solution practices will deliver to you the power to influence others.

If you want to learn better selling techniques there is no point in just learning the words. You need to understand why and how the words, the communications work. You can't sing a song if you only know the words and not the music. Without really understanding the material you cannot comprehend or successfully put the necessary steps into action. Then again, while it is important to know all the techniques by heart, they are of no use unless you *put them into action, evaluate the results and understand the outcome.* And then have another go. This set up, progression of learning better skills, is the same whether you are learning to sell, play golf, drive a car, learn medicine… or whatever.

- To improve your selling or your golf you must evaluate both your positive and negative outcomes. Do not just consider what went wrong but consider how and what went right. There are a lot of positives to be learned from noting what went right.

- Improving your skills happens by repeating actions that produce positive rather than negative results.

LEARNING NEW SKILLS

Understanding the ideas.

You learn best when you really understand new ideas and do so in such a way that the ideas make sense to you. When something makes sense it is usually accepted and retained. Therefore, do not go past anything unless you have grasped it and can see why and how it works. You do not have to agree with everything initially and that's fine. It is even wise to argue and debate new ideas as doing that can help the learning process. So until you GET IT, do not move on, keep working at fully understanding a particular proposition. If you are having trouble with it, seek help. A truly independent adult person is never afraid to say, "I don't know," and is always willing to ask for help.

When learning new skills it is inevitable that you will need to discard some habitual bad ones. This involves change, and change is always a little scary and fear hinders learning. Most people agree that things constantly change and yet find it hard to change their practices, to let in new ideas and skills and to do so intentionally.

Why? Because with change, immediate resistance rises within. In truth, change is rarely welcomed because it always *seems* to imply extra work.

In this busy world, for most of us it is easy to throw new ideas away because our current mindset is likely to be a touch lazy, a little scared, and is already full of things we need to do. True enough. But a change can also bring needed relief from being, say, too busy. Change always seems, and sometimes is, hard to implement. This is as true for an organization as it is for an individual. If understanding, commitment, intention and a bit of courage are not present we soon forget what we have learned, even if we thought that it was a good thing.

So, the mind thinks, "Oh no, here is more work. I am asked to do more when in fact...." Yet the good news is that we are never bored or depressed while learning something new. We do get bored – or what seems like it – if we do not understand what is being offered because we cut out and turn off. True, we might even get a bit stressed at having to work at it. But if we do it with the right attitude, learn something we want or need, it all changes into a wonderful process.

You cannot refill a full cup.

> When we are actually learning new skills we don't get bored we get excited.

The learning process is usually easy and fun for children, but harder for adults because they often feel they should already know everything. This is the 'as if you knew' type of thinking and you need to keep an eye on this. 'As if you knew' is the reaction many people have during the learning process and I know that just by looking at the faces in workshops. This sort of thinking switches off your receptivity and it is a big problem because your adult ego

LEARNING NEW SKILLS

wants to pretend it already 'sort of knows' things. Some people suffer from this more than others.

When you are learning, do it with an open childlike curiosity. There will be time later to accept or discard whatever you have read or heard. Be open to what you read here. Once you have gone through the book twice then you can debate and decide on various points. For now, just be open to it as you would be to reading a good novel or seeing a favourite movie. Unless you are certain you have understood, it is better to admit you have not and ask for further explanation. Read it again, ask your fellow salespeople or a mate, wife, husband, whoever.

It is nearly impossible to achieve lasting personal or business change all by yourself. That is why you might need expert input, teachers and people with experience. It can also be easier to learn and change when you share the experience with trusted others. It helps if they are involved in the same, or a similar, process. Discuss the material, try it on each other, and get feedback. Do this at work and at home. But be wary of negative nay sayers – people who are knockers of everything.

Take action – try it out.

If you do not act on new input, if you do not put it into practice then nothing has been learned and no improvement can result. Taking well-considered actions may result in great success or it may not. However, if you have taken in the new learning properly, it is unlikely that a disaster will follow. Disasters usually happen when actions have been based on incorrect or insufficient input and you have reacted, without proper know-how.

Take action, use what you have learned. Look at what the result is and try it again and again and see what it brings. Your actions will need to be changed and massaged to adapt to the various situations you find yourself in. This now brings us to some important ideas.

COMPETENCY, SKILLS, EXPERTISE; THE STAGES OF LEARNING

To explain the learning process a bit further we need to look at the various stages of learning. What follows here is partially taken from the ideas of Neuro-Linguistic-Programming (NLP) with my alterations and additions. Understanding the four phases of competence will bring some clarity as to what stage your current skills are.

1. Unaware or Unconscious Non-Competence

Babies do not know that they don't know. For example, they do not even comprehend that they know how to suck on the breast. They have an innate biological skill for this however, they do not consciously know they are doing it.

Babies do not know how to drive a car or cook food and they do not comprehend that they don't know, or that there is anything to know. The term unaware non-competence is used to describe this.

2. Conscious non-competence

As we grow, we increase our skills and knowledge. A six-year-old child probably knows that fire burns and that although parents can drive cars children cannot. The six year old knows that mum can cook, but he/she can't, or that their older brother can ride a bike and swim, but they cannot. The six year old knows that they have not yet learned how to do these things and won't know until they are taught. However, they are aware now that those skills exist and may be learned. This is the stage called aware or conscious non-competence.

3. Conscious competence

In this phase, say in the teenage years, we learn to drive a car. When we learn to start driving we make many mistakes and for a while feel a bit sweaty and nervous on the road. Nevertheless, we know that with practice we will get a license and will be able to drive. This is conscious competence. We know what to do and how to do it, at least up to a point. This is the skill level most salespeople use when selling. It is what most of us probably recognize as competence, but there is more.

4. Instinctive or automatic competence

The automatic competence phase of learning is what we are vitally interested in. Most adults do not need to think about how to multiply 5 by 5, or about how to drive the car or how to swim. Imagine if a surgeon didn't automatically know what to do when operating or if a car mechanic had to stop and look at instructions all the time. There are many professions where people simply cannot work unless they have at least some 'automatic competence.'

Selling also calls for automatic competence, even though automatic competence is less vital for the salesperson than for the surgeon who has a belly open. In the selling profession most people have a kind of partial know-how. The knowledge base is rarely good enough and rarely automatic competence or what comes out as automatic actually is bad selling technique.

Most selling practices contain four or six seemingly easy steps. Everyone *sort* of knows some, or even all of the steps, but it is rare for salespeople to know the steps well enough so that they can recite them by heart; the first step is needed if we really want to do things in the best possible way.

Salespeople without automatic competence just flounder through sales presentations. Once we have real automatic competence we can be flexible and creative and can then do what is vital. That is not just to ask questions and supply answers, but find the right questions and the right answers in order to get a sale and to make a customer.

Without automatic competence every slightly difficult situation can become stressful, or at the least, boring and meaningless. In the trickier than usual selling situations we need to be able to bring forth the right procedures and the correct ways to communicate with ease to be successful. Automatic competence is not doing things in parrot fashion. Rather it is the ability to intelligently handle whatever happens during a sales presentation. It is an automatic, instinctive know-how that never lets us down and is easy to produce.

CHAPTER 3

SELLING SOLUTIONS – A SORT OF 'STAIRCASE' MODEL

1. QUESTIONING TECHNIQUES ARE THE 'UMBRELLA' OF SUCCESSFUL COMMUNICATIONS

Now we are ready to look at the actual steps of selling, the process and progress of a *focused piece of communication we call selling*. There are few things more important in selling than finding out what a particular customer wants and needs. How else can we find 'solutions' or have any chance of influencing others but by asking them good questions?

I asked camera salespeople at a workshop whether they knew what their customers wanted. Much laughter resulted: "a camera... to take pictures...to show off" people said. Fair enough up to a point but why do they need the camera? What do they want to take pictures of? Do they want to be professional photographers?

SELLING IS NOT *JUST* TELLING

Do they have perhaps a new grandchild? Are they interested in some artistic aspect of the lanes of Melbourne?

To know answers we have to ask questions and most salespeople are rather bad at asking good questions; they tell not sell. Telling is not question asking, selling **is**. The first and most important communication and sales skill to master is asking questions good questions. The first half of the secret of successful selling is appropriate use of good questioning techniques.

> Appropriate question asking is like an 'umbrella' it covers and contains all the steps of good selling and of satisfactory private communications with others.

To find out about anything you need to ask questions. Obvious huh? Everyone will say that they know something about question asking techniques. Fair enough, but so many people neither use nor understand appropriate questioning techniques, a curious fact given that communicating with others is very reliant on asking questions. Most salespeople do not ask lots of questions, and when they do, many of them are useless, inappropriate or wrongly timed.

> The selling steps build a structure that help to always ask the right questions at the right time. Conversely, using appropriate questions helps to build the selling steps.

Of course, no one can tell you exactly what questions you need to use in your situation. By following the structure of the selling steps this will become more and more obvious and easy. You will need to put in time and effort to find the correct and profitable questions in your particular sales setting. What style of question is needed at what point is important and you must use the method

SELLING SOLUTIONS – A SORT OF 'STAIRCASE' MODEL

intentionally. *Ask the right questions and you will get the right answers.*

Ask the wrong ones and guess what...?

> **There are only two kinds of questions possible in the English language: open questions or closed ones.**

Every question you can possibly ask is either open or closed. A closed question is one that may be, and usually is answered by a simple yes or no. *Closed questions ask for a decision.* For example:

Question: "Do you want to go for a walk?"
Possible answers: "Yes" or "No"

Question: "Can you use this?"
Answer: "Yes" or "No"

Question: " Would you like to buy this?"
Answer: "Yes" or "No"

As you can see, closed questions tend to invite a yes or no answer, even though the customer responding might elaborate. Closed questions usually start with a *'do, can, will, would'* type of word. You may get more of an answer than yes or no, but a decision is asked for by you and this can cut short the communication. At the same time closed questions move the conversation in a direction, which, in the selling situation, may be awkward, unwanted or badly timed. If you ask a closed question at the wrong time, you can alienate the customer as they may feel you are being pushy and are in too much of a hurry. For example, if you ask the following closed question before the customer is convinced: "So would you like to buy this car?" you are likely to get a negative answer because your timing is wrong. Your request for a decision is too early. You have created a problem. It is always harder to get the customer to make a full reversal from a negative direction.

To find out if your customer is interested in a product, always use an open question.

Open questions don't pressure the customer. For example, "So, what do you think about this car?" or, "What colour would you prefer?"

> Some closed questions are truly odd. For example, in an episode of the TV series Seinfeld, Jerry, probably the best philosopher of our time, was exploring just this situation. He was wondering what parents expected from a child when they asked a closed question like: "Do you want a slap on your face?" What could a kid answer? If he says yes, he is cheeky, and if he says no, he is asking for more trouble.

Chances are that closed questions may close the communication. They are not the way to go if you need more information, or if you are trying to see if you are on the right track for a sale. However, there are more points to consider here. For example, if I ask whether this book is helping you, your answer may be yes or no or not sure. None of these answers give me much feedback, so I need to ask more questions, and these need to be open questions. Let's say you answered, "Yes, this book is helping me." I still do not have much information. I need to follow up by asking "How" or "In what way" does it help. 'How' and 'What' are some of the key words when asking open questions.

If I have changed my question to "What is it in this book that is helpful?" you cannot simply say yes or no, you are likely, after some thought, to offer me some more information. The open question invites customers to provide further information upon which you may be able to build, even if the information the customer has given is negative. For instance, if you said, "No, this book is not

SELLING SOLUTIONS – A SORT OF 'STAIRCASE' MODEL

helping me much" then I could ask "What were you expecting or hoping to be helped with?" Or "What sort of information would be more helpful to you?" To this, you might answer by explaining to me the subject or situations you need to learn about. The right solution for the current 'customer' will become obvious if the correct questions are asked. This will also lead to doing the actual sales presentation in the right way.

Open questions are always answered by more information.

Open questions give you new information and a new 'hook' from which you can create more questions and maintain the conversation in a positive way.

The key words for open questions are How, What, When, Where, Why, Which and Who.

These are all questions asking for input beyond yes or no. Some examples are: "How do you feel about this?" "What do you think?" "How would this help?" "In what way is that a problem?" These questions cannot be answered with just a yes or a no. However, be careful with 'why ' questions as these can sound a bit pushy or aggressive. Salespeople believe that they already ask a lot of questions, but how focused and how productive are they, even if this is true? Mostly it is not; salespeople are notoriously bad at asking customers good or even any questions. What questions does the customer want to hear? The skill is to intentionally ask the questions you need to move the interaction in the direction you want it to go. That direction will also be satisfactory to your customer because the questions will be about his/her wants, needs and interests. In thirty years of teaching people how to sell, how to improve personal communications and sort out their relationship issues, I have come across many people who ask lots of questions without realizing which style of questioning they were using – open or closed. I find, to this day, that most people have a lack of clarity about this issue. Perhaps from your personal experience, and certainly from your buying experiences, you might recognize how infuriating it is when people ask you, the customer, no questions, too many questions, not enough or the wrong questions at the wrong time. The wrong questions create tension and argument and too many questions in a row can sound aggressive. Not enough questions can suggest a lack of interest in the other person. On the other hand, nothing makes people feel better than when **they are asked appropriate questions that show interest in what they are saying.**

(I wish I knew all this when I was a young fella at parties bumbling around, not knowing what to say to the girls of my dreams!) The actual questions you ask must be relevant and aimed at making a sale. For example, asking a customer who is interested in buying a red car whether he had seen any car races may be irrelevant, or it might not be. Asking whether he intends to use it on dirt roads, or for towing, are likely to be relevant if discussing a large car. Asking if she is married is likely to be a bad question, but rephrased to "How many of you in the family to fit into the car?" is a reasonable one. When selling, you need to keep your questions relevant and focused even if your discussion or chitchat has taken a slightly different turn. And yes, even questions about footy are mostly irrelevant. Fake friendliness won't really get you a sale.

> You cannot and will not ask good questions without the awareness of knowing what type of questions you are asking, what result each type of question brings, and when it is appropriate to use open or closed questions. This is vital. At the end of your sales presentation is the best time to ask a closed question in order to test finalize the sale but... wait there is more!

How do we get to ask 'good' questions?

SELLING SOLUTIONS – A SORT OF 'STAIRCASE' MODEL

Always show interest in what a buyer or anyone else, for that matter, wants. That is the art of communicating. It is after this, and only if appropriate, that you can then move onto influencing others and taking them in a different direction. This is your job at work and in life, at times. Well meant questions mean well and others will hear them that way. Ordinary, fake, boring or unfocused questions will be hard and they will not work. In selling, you need to know your product, the market place, and have some understanding of people (more about this last important point in another part of the book). Questions must aim and progress towards the goal of making a sale. Pointless questions diffuse the issue. By listening to customers properly, you will learn where you need to go and what are the right questions to ask, giving you the right focus. Good open questions will bring information from your customer and provide you with a 'hook', a jump off point that will tell you what your next good question might be.

Are all open questions good?	No.
Are all closed questions bad?	No.

The idea is to use a mix, but they must be well timed and appropriate and lead somewhere. It is a matter of knowing which style of question to use and when. Whether you ask an open or a closed question depends at which stage the sale is.

> In my younger days as a salesman in a Sydney camera store we were selling the new Polaroid instant cameras aimed at the younger yuppie market. A particular model was named 'The Swinger." An older lady came in and asked, "Have you got them instant films love?
>
> My daughter is getting married." I nodded and asked her if it was for a 'Swinger.' She furrowed her brow and answered, "Good heavens no, it's for my husband..."

SELLING IS NOT *JUST* TELLING

Early in a sale you need to establish what the customer wants. *You need research questions.* For example you need to find out:

- What products or services have you seen or considered so far?

- What do you expect from the product or service?

- Have you purchased from our company before?

As the right questions and get the right answers...

There may be several other good questions depending on your selling situation but these three are a must for starters. Salespeople generally do far too little research of the customer's wants.

> In the early stage of the sale you should ask more open questions because you need information to find out what you need to know about your customer.

SELLING SOLUTIONS – A SORT OF 'STAIRCASE' MODEL

An example of a bad early question, used by nearly all retail sales staff, is to ask the customer how much they wish to spend. Though this information is necessary, price range will become apparent from the responses you get from your proper research questions. Years ago I did a survey of my staff as to what were the most important customer research questions. Many came back with the following: "Can I help you?" and "What can I help you with?" and the like. After that they were kind of stuck.

Finding out the customer's needs is the most important step in any sale.

There was an old-fashioned sales training film that was dramatically titled "The Last Three Feet" and this film focused on something of absolute importance. The 'last three feet' refers to your first meeting with the customer face to face. Mess that up by either bad body language or the wrong questions, or no questions or bad listening techniques and your goose is cooked.

Salespeople agree that finding out the customer's needs is of great importance.

This seems and is obvious. Although everyone agrees, very few salespeople get it right. Very few salespeople in retail or in commercial situations ever get past more than a couple of questions regarding the customer's needs. I suggest that in retail particularly, it should be an aim to ask at least five, and up to nine questions before proceeding to the product demonstration stage.

In industrial sales or services, or on high-ticket items such as cars, even more questions may be needed. How many to ask depends on the complexity of the product and the customer. I hasten to add that your research questions are likely to be not only of a technical nature, but even more importantly, should be about the customer's aspirations, needs, ideas, dreams, worries, past history, etc.

SELLING IS NOT *JUST* TELLING

When you are at the 'show and tell' stage, demonstrating the product, you still need mainly open questions to constantly check that you are on the right track. Later, when you get to close the sale, you need a decision so you might change to closed questions. All this is equally true also in personal relationships. Many arguments and much unhappiness occur because partners, parents, friends ask the wrong style of question at the wrong time. Imagine that you wish to stay home and make love while your partner wants to go out to a nightclub. If you both just state what you want there is a gulf, and resentment builds. You ask a question like: "Do you want to stay home?" (closed) and your partner says "No." Well, that is the end of that. You may then try to convince your partner otherwise. Your next attempt is an open but misguided question like, "Why don't you want to go out?" And you get a lot of answers you might not wish to hear. A better approach may be to ask. "How would it be if we…?" There is a potential element of compromise to open questions. That element suggests that perhaps we can both have a 'sale' – so to speak.

In the selling situation the same applies. The idea is to use both open and closed questions appropriately. Remember that you are not out to win an argument, but to achieve a good solution/outcome. That usually happens only if and when both parties find an outcome close to what they desire. The win-win scenario is often talked about but it is quite misunderstood. Amos Oz, an Israeli writer, explained that win-win actually means that while both parties may not win and get all that they would like, both parties should win a good enough outcome. Apply this to any international tension, to an argument at home, and certainly to dealing with a customer and you will see what he was saying.

The right questioning technique works with children, adults, men and women, and even within your own mind when trying to solve issues and make decisions. Just think what happens when you are debating something within yourself. If you ask yourself closed questions you get short answers, most of which is information you already know. If you ask yourself open questions you may find that you will need to answer yourself with a longer explanation, or 'story' which may reveal something new to you. You need to think about and feel what is going on within. Once that is done, a closed question will tell you whether to act (yes) or not act (no).

2. 'SUMMARY LISTENING' IS POSSIBLY THE MOST INFLUENTIAL COMMUNICATION TOOL

Summary listening is dynamic and effective listening and it is the other half of the secret of being really good at selling and communicating. There are a few simple rules to follow:

- Give your attention to others when they speak.

- Stop your 'inner' dialogue; don't just hear, but really listen.

- Let the customer do most of the talking. Do not break in too often while others are talking.

- Accept what is said, do not challenge it, for now.

- Understand emotive words, but do not get hooked by them.

- Put yourself in the customer's place.

You can do all the above by employing three simple ideas when it is your turn to respond:

- Summarize briefly what you've heard from the customer and what you have discussed or agreed to so far.

- Ask for confirmation that you have understood correctly.

- Consider the information you are given and note what it tells you.

Nothing could be simpler. Yet hardly anyone does it right. Why is this? Generally, because your mind races ahead and wants to put out what you think. Another reason might be that although you heard the customer's words you have not actually 'listened' or understood. If this is the case then don't be afraid to ask again for clarification.[1]

Your summary of what you have heard from the customer should be brief and address the main points: "So, what I think I have heard from you is that a regular service call and reliability is important and that the capacity has to be at last 58% etc. ...so, have I got it right so far?"

Leave out other details, extraneous ideas, chitchat and issues that need not be discussed at this point. For example, in the early stages you might sail past the 'what will it cost' issue for the moment. You might leave out addressing the issue that thirty years ago a particular brand of TV they had was no good, or that her husband only likes black ones rather than silver ones. Acknowledge it all, keep it in mind, but move past it for the time being.

Using summary listening and proper questioning gives you time to accurately establish what product the customer might be happy with. It will clarify what really matters to your client. Often a customer may have an idea of what he/she would like, but the particular item or deal may not be the best for them. Alternatively,

---

[1] By the way, I think that most of us who hated school when young, or did not do well, were suffering from a case of being afraid to ask again and again for clarification. If that happens, a child loses confidence and is left behind so that more complex learning is nearly impossible.

you find that they have an interest in doing something with this product that another product may do better. Your careful listening skills will give you the opportunity to offer more suitable products. The fact that many customers are not sure what they want or need, is one of the reasons why many people will never buy on the Internet when it comes to products with technical features and benefits. But perhaps the main reason for employing the summary listening is that doing *it is including the customer!*

One reason why summary listening and the right questions are so important is that using these techniques stops you from doing your usual solo performance and includes the customer. And hey, all customers will like that. Everyone wants to feel included in making any sort of deal. Everyone wants to feel that the salesperson is showing interest in what they have to say. Everyone wants to feel they have been seen and heard. Everybody likes to feel that what they have to say matters, and it certainly does matter. Surely this is true for all of us. Otherwise, we are all ships passing each other in the dark night on open seas, unseen, unheard and with no real communication.[2]

SHOW YOUR CONCERNED FACE

What you actually need to do is simply this: listen to what the customer is saying using your ears, eyes and body. Wait for their answers if you asked questions and *look like you are listening*. I say 'look like' because it is vitally important that your body language actually conveys that you are paying attention. The customer must be able to see your 'concerned' face, and 'concerned' is certainly

---

[2] It is worthy to note that the divorce statistics are full of people who said that the primary reason for the break-up of their relationship was that they did not feel they were understood, considered or properly heard. Usually both parties said much the same thing.

what you ought to be. After all, you want to earn more money and become successful at whatever you do.

The third point of summary listening is to *consider the information you are given as well as the information that is not said.* What people say is fairly obvious, but what is not said may tell you a lot more. There is 'sub-text' in what people tell us. The information you get by sub text can be vitally important. You may draw some assumptions from sub text, but you always need to check these assumptions with the customer. That is easy to do, just ask whether blah blah and ping pong was what they meant. Again, all this will further improve your agreement/engagement with this customer.

SELLING SOLUTIONS – A SORT OF 'STAIRCASE' MODEL

HOW SUB TEXT WORKS FOR YOU

Let's face it, some customers will not directly or clearly tell you what they mean or how they feel about what you are offering. 'Sub-text' is what is implied by words and body language. As the old cliché tells us, 'a picture tells a thousand words.' Pay good attention to sub-text, body language and words used by the client. It will tell you more than what is being verbalized.

Imagine that you are a salesperson in a camera store in the city. Your customer tells you that she wants a video camera because the family is going on holiday to Fiji. She tells you that she has never used a video camera before, so she wants something simple and easy to use without too many features; a very common scenario. At this point you might ask when they are travelling and who will be using the camera. She tells you that they are going next week and everyone in the family will use the camera. You ask if she has seen anything so far. She tells you that she has been looking around a bit and has seen the You Beaut model ST at another store in Frankston.

You need to consider what has been said in two ways. Firstly, listen to the information she has given you and then interpret the sub-text underlying the information. You have to be careful about interpreting what the customer says. Using the listening techniques you check whether what you think you've just heard is accurate. First, summarize briefly what you've heard from the customer and what you have discussed or agreed to so far. Ask for confirmation that you have got it right. Consider the information you were given and what else it tells you.

I've said this already but it is so important: the customer sees that they have been heard and that's got to be a good thing. Even more importantly, when you use the listening techniques you get 'agreement' and that has started you on the *agreement staircase* of getting a sale. OR the customer partly disagrees with your summary. If so, use that as a chance to clarify something you may well have missed. What develops is trust and clear communication that makes customers feel like you are a good person to buy from.

Now back to our example. So what else do we know now? There is a lot of sub-text in our example. You heard that she has children which may mean you need to ask questions about whether the video camera might also be used to take movies of the sports the kids do, and so on. She says 'yes' young John is an ace footy player. Aha... What does it tell you? It suggests that a camera with a better zoom ability may be helpful. There is more yet. You know the family is going on holidays to Fiji. What does that say? I reckon this family is not on the bread line since they are going on an expensive holiday. So, do you try to sell them something very dear? That is not the point, but your realizing that cost may not be the ultimate consideration is important. If you can convince her that she will be better off with a camera capable of more zooming power, the extra cost won't stop her from buying it. You would have also heard, because you asked what she has seen so far, that she has been shopping around and has seen model ST. This information gives you a lead on the price range she is willing to consider. Another piece of subtext is that she has already done some shopping around so she may be ready to settle on a purchase today. Assume that in her shopping till now she has not been convinced; because she has not yet made a purchase. That may mean that she has not yet seen anything that she liked or that the other stores have not convinced her to buy.

More sub-text yet: It sounds like she lives a fair way from the city as she mentioned shopping in the suburbs. That could suggest that if you do not get the sale now she may not come back all the way into the city, unless you make a very good impression on her.

SELLING SOLUTIONS – A SORT OF 'STAIRCASE' MODEL

You see how much info we have gained already, but would you believe it, there is more still. However, at this is a point you might stop and apply the summary listening techniques again. Summarize what has been said and ask for agreement so far. At any time during a sale it is a good thing to stop and very briefly summarize what and where you are in your negotiations. Each time the client agrees, you are closer to a sale. For example, you might proceed like this: "Sounds like a great holiday coming up. By what you have told me so far you want a camera for family movies and to film the kids sporting activities. I should show you something with a reasonably powerful zoom lens and yet easy to use. You've seen cameras in the $900-1000 price range and you seem comfortable in that price range. Have I got that right?" The customer will likely agree to your summary given that all you've done so far is to reflect what she told you. Now you may proceed to getting more information. Perhaps you could ask whether she has had a video camera before, and whether she has purchased from this store before. Is the size and weight of the camera a consideration? And so on. Once you have this information you might proceed to offer a couple of choices, one of which may or may not be the model she has already seen and move on to demonstrating a camera or two. Let's consider that, in answer to your summary as to whether we're on the right track, the customer says, "No, not exactly." You need to probe a touch further. Perhaps she was impressed by the model ST she was shown, but she does not actually want to spend that much money. This may be sub text once again because she hasn't actually said that the cost of the model ST was a bit high. Alternatively, she may have said 'no, not exactly' because she is concerned that you left out in your summary her request for a very small, light camera or something else.

Whether the customer agrees with your summary or not, either way s/he will still feel that you are properly interested in what they want to purchase. Unless that is, your summary is completely wrong.

All the way through the demonstration of the product stage recheck that the customer is comfortable with what you've shown and said. Take care in your choice of wording here. Don't ask if they have understood – that sounds like a put down. Ask whether using this camera seems easy enough, or simply, "How does that sound?" "How do you feel about this so far?" or words to that effect. If you get agreement as the sale proceeds then at the end of your presentation all that will be left is to ask a closed question to get a decision. "Have we found what you're looking for?" If the answer is "Yes" then ask only "Will it be cash or credit card?"

> "You don't get a second chance to make a first impression." (H.G.Seebach of Dupont Corporation).

PRACTICING GOOD COMMUNICATION SKILLS

Practice the techniques at home and at work, and plan to do it on purpose! Initially you may feel a touch awkward and selfconscious planning such practice. Remember that everyone is already asking questions and listening. All you are practicing in a focused way is skills you already know, but now you are doing it with intention, commitment and attention. The right words will come eventually, and the whole thing will become second nature or automatic competence. To try out these ideas, think about appropriate questions that focus on a situation. If you are going to try it at home, and I recommend you do, keep in mind the following story from one of my workshops.

A young and enthusiastic new salesperson, George, eagerly listened to what I had to say about all the above and went home determined to try the questioning techniques on his new wife. The following day at the workshop he related this story.

SELLING SOLUTIONS – A SORT OF 'STAIRCASE' MODEL

George arrived home: *"Honey I'm home. How was your day?"* After a hug she usually said that her day was good or bad and to this he would usually answer by saying what his day had been like. But this particular evening, having learned his new techniques, he was determined to do things differently by showing his interest and changing the way they communicated.

"How was your day, honey?" George asked.

"I had a terrible day actually," she answered.

"Aha," thought George. This is my chance to ask good open questions. *"What made it so terrible, darling?"*

She answered, *"Oh the boss came in all day putting more and more work on my desk. The coffee machine was broken and my computer was playing up. On top of that your mother rang to ask if I could pick her up and take her to the doctor after work when she knows that it is my basketball practice night. As if that wasn't enough, after I took her home I slipped over and hurt my ankle because I was in a hurry."*

"Oh dear," said George. *"I think we had better sit down because I'd like to hear more."*

They sat down and she started answering his open questions. After a few minutes she suddenly stopped and moving back from him with a drawn and suspicious face she asked, "What's all this about? Have you been playing up?"

George quickly managed to explain to his wife that he had learned at his sales course that using more open questions showed interest, and he was just trying to practice being a better communicator. The story had a happy ending and an interesting footnote. While George's wife welcomed the idea of George's attempt to be a better communicator she made the point that

SELLING IS NOT *JUST* TELLING

she hoped that his interest in talking to her was genuine and not just a chance to practice technique.

Good questions do not happen by accident. You have to think about them, try them and ask yourself what worked and what did not. You have to work out why you asked what you did, by way of considering what you were trying to achieve. You may find all this planning and thinking a bit artificial at first, but as you go on using the ideas, it becomes easy, like anything else you practice. To learn anything you need to be deliberate and persevere.

> If you don't know where you are going you are liable to end up nowhere.

THE 'SO WHAT?' TEST

A good question to ask yourself, before asking anyone anything or taking any action is: "So what?" What are you trying to achieve. You need to be able to rationally and sensibly answer the "so what?" test. In other words, why are you asking a particular question or taking a particular action, and what are you expecting to achieve? For example, the customer tells you that he is short on space in his office. To make the point that your machine takes up less space than the one offered by your competitor is a good thing, but it is unnecessary to ask if saving space is of interest to him because that is already obvious. So leave pointless questions, open or closed, out. It is better to ask nothing than bad questions, but there are always good ones, if you give it some thought. Learn from yourself by quietly rethinking one of your past sales presentations. It is great to do this in writing. Once you have it all down, look at where good pointed questions might fit, always with a view to what and how your question might achieve the desired goal.

When the customer says that s/he wants a camera that is easy to use it is worthwhile to find out what they really mean by easy. Asking this will answer the 'so what' question; it will tell you the customer's level of expertise. However, if you were dealing with a professional rally car driver there would be no point in asking if he is interested in safer tyres. When you ask good questions the answers provide you with information you need. If you don't get new info and/or agreement then perhaps your question was not useful.

One other issue about the content of questions is not to ask too many good questions about the same point. That is, do not labour on and on. So you have asked some good questions and received good answers, now what? The key to great selling, at this and many other stages, is to sum up what the customer said and what has been discussed so far and ask for agreement. Once this is done

SELLING IS NOT *JUST* TELLING

you are offering what everyone wants – *benefits and solutions that bring satisfaction.*

CHAPTER 4

THE AGREEMENT SUMMARY OF SELLING – A SERIES OF STEPS

MONEY DOESN'T COME FROM THE SALE OF PRODUCTS, IT COMES FROM CUSTOMERS

Agreement Summary Selling is a series of steps. You start at the bottom of the staircase, and follow a sequence of 'selling steps' to get to the top that is a successful sale and an ongoing customer relationship. Many sales and marketing people might make a sale, but rarely gain a customer. To make a sale, to get to your goal or aim, you need to decide on the actions you need to take to move forward (as many politicians put it...) For successful selling you need, above all else, an absolutely firm grip on the Selling Steps. You need what I termed earlier as instinctive or *automatic competence*.

A sale is a sale, but a 'customer' is someone who comes back to buy from you and recommends you and your business to others. Even if you do not get the sale, but have done the right things, you have at least impressed someone sufficiently for them to think: "This salesperson is helpful and genuine. I will come back to this business again."

THE SELLING STEPS ARE THE FRAMEWORKS FOR ACHIEVING A SALE

To this you add your personality, communication skills and the features and benefits of your company, as well as that of the product you are offering. I cannot state it too often: knowledge of the selling steps is absolutely necessary. Those who do not use them consciously are not professionals. Those who are professionals jump sometimes from one stage to another leaving out some of the steps, if it is appropriate. However, take care. What step you leave out may well be the very step you find hardest to do and need most to learn. Without knowing the steps like two plus two equals four, you simply cannot be a professional salesperson.

> Do you have to know what to say or how to proceed no matter what your customer says? Yes. You have to know how to proceed well enough to feel and act confident in just about any selling situation.

THE AGREEMENT SUMMARY OF SELLING – A SERIES OF STEPS

If you don't know where you're going you are liable to end up nowhere.

HOW WELL DO YOU KNOW THE 'SELLING STEPS'?

There are only a few steps to selling, and these seem simple enough. If it were that simple, everyone would be great at selling. In fact most salespeople, I am sorry to say, are at best, counter-hoppers and rather dismal at their trade. Selling can be as smooth and easy as riding a bicycle once you are competent. It depends on whether you understand and use the selling steps properly. Once you have real understanding, once it is all bedded in and you have reached the 'automatic competence' stage, selling is easy, simple and satisfying in spite of the fact that you cannot win them all. But this is when selling becomes fun, less stressful and very, very profitable. This stage, this proficiency is no different from anything you have learned to do reasonably well. When you first begin to learn something it can be a chore and confusing. Once you know and experience doing things right, the know-how beds in and the fun starts.

Some salespeople think they 'sort of know' some of the selling steps. These are the 'as if' thinkers I discussed before. When you fumble around, when you do not know what to say next or how to progress, when you stand there hoping the customer will give you the nod, then selling is stressful and tricky and likely to not achieve a sale. Professional selling has a sense of friendly and comfortable connection to a total stranger, a sense of having been of service.

I cautioned to be careful about leaving out any of the steps. That is what the amateurs often do. Take the easy way and sometimes things become hard. Strange isn't it? But when we take what seems at least initially the hard way, things often finish up being easy.

Get to know the steps word for word. That is easy enough. BUT BUT BUT not only learn the words, understand what is meant. It all has to make sense to you. Try out the steps and evaluate your procedure each time you sell over the next few weeks. When you are comfortable with all the steps and have thoroughly evaluated what worked well for you then you can move on to become familiar with the finer, more subtle details. The next stage is where you adapt your know-how to suit your personality type and style, situation, product and company. That is why later on I willexplore more about how and why an individual operates as a person buying or selling.

AGREEMENT SUMMARY SELLING IS CUSTOMER FOCUSED SELLING, IT IS NOT JUST 'TELLING'

If you are not centred on your customer in a focused way, you are not providing service and you are certainly not selling. Your customer is, after all, the vital ingredient when making a sale. Almost everyone has had a bad experience when buying fine

THE AGREEMENT SUMMARY OF SELLING – A SERIES OF STEPS

products. Usually this is due to the seller's inability to say and do the right things. On the other hand, people have also had very satisfactory buying experiences as a result of the way they were served, helped and communicated with. Ask yourself these few important questions:

- Do you have the kind of product this customer is really asking for? You need to clarify what your customer needs and wants.

- Do you have enough expertise to talk about the products, in order to meet the customer's needs and wants? Clearly, product knowledge is a must.

- What is the competition in your area and what is going on in the market place? It is nearly impossible to be a professional if you are not aware of the competition.

- Has this customer purchased from your store/company before? Find out, because if they have, then they probably had a good buying experience.

- Which particular products does your company prefer to sell and why?

> Confidence equals competence.
> Competence is confidence.

Confidence comes from knowing what you are talking about. However, confidence is not just knowledge; it's about demonstrating your knowledge in ways that relate to the customer's needs. The best way to relate to the customer's needs is to use the communication techniques. Customers like a confident seller and they can smell a fake.

THE FIVE EASY STEPS OF SELLING EVERYONE KNOWS...DON'T THEY?

Yeah, sort of. But 'sort of' is like being a 'bit pregnant' – nonsense. Either you know the steps by heart, which would mean having that 'automatic competence' or you do not. The five easy steps to selling I refer to as *Agreement Summary Selling* are:

Step 1   Meet and greet
Step 2   Research your customer
Step 3   Set objectives
Step 4   Sell Benefits not features
Step 5   Close the Sale

Now let's look at each point in some more detail. There are only five simple steps that truly are, or will become easy if you know what you are doing.

STEP 1. MEET AND GREET

Everyone knows how to greet people in personal life and you do not keep friends waiting without saying 'hello.' However, many salespeople don't greet potential customers immediately. A lot of retail salespeople tell me that they are concerned about approaching customers as soon as they walk into a store as that feels like they are pouncing on the customer. I don't think this true. Customers want to be acknowledged and if they are just looking and don't wish to talk they will say so. Immediate recognition by the salesperson simply conveys that when the customer is ready the salesperson is available to assist. Most customers will wait for a reasonable time so long as they have been greeted and assured that someone will serve them soon.

The crux of the matter depends on your opening line. If you say 'Can I help you?' that is a closed question, easy for the customer

THE AGREEMENT SUMMARY OF SELLING – A SERIES OF STEPS

to answer with a yes or no. Turning this into an open question by asking 'How can I help you?' is more likely to get a better response. Body language, opening words and tone are what is important. Personally, I hate the "How are you today?" approach, and I believe that most customers are happy to be greeted with a "Good morning, won't be long" or something similar. Do not ever address customers using inappropriate words like 'mate' 'buddy' and 'love' (ugh!)

In the more commercial selling situation, where you have an appointment with a client, the actual greeting is less of a problem, but how and what you say in the first couple of moments can set the tone for the rest of the interview. In these situations my strong suggestion is that your opening lines should focus on the research stage, the next step in agreement summary selling.

Never say no? Well, not to start with, unless you are asked for shoes and you are in the computer business. Whatever the customer asks for, you should never just say "No, sorry we don't have, or sell that brand" even if that is the case. There is always a better way to put it such as "Yes that's a good product but I think we have an interesting alternative." Or "any reason why you are looking for that brand or model particularly?" If a customer insists on a particular brand you do not sell, then of course you must let it go gracefully. Some salespeople respond with an instant "No" if an enquiry is made such as "Can you fix my mobile phone by tomorrow?" Even if you cannot do that, the worst thing to do is to immediately say no. Instead, find out in what, if any, other way you can help. Find alternative ways of helping before you give up.

The damn phone? (It is your selling partner!)

The telephone is often your first contact with a customer. How they perceive your greeting, tone of voice, and what you say will either put them off or it will give you a chance to sell your product. Ordinary salespeople say that phone inquiries are a pain, time consuming and stressful. It is certainly not the actual telephone that is upsetting to use, is it? After all, most of us will happily chat on the phone to family and friends, and usually for too long. Clearly it is not the phone we dislike, nor talking to people we want to speak to. Somehow, we find talking to a customer on the phone tricky at times. We say it is because we are busy and because the calls interrupt us. But hey, look, it is your job calling you each time the phone rings to tell you about things you need to and should want to know. Perhaps it is your phone technique and attitude that is at fault?

Many salespeople have no real phone technique beyond saying hello. Sure every salesperson knows the basics of phone usage. Most think that you use the phone as you might at home. This isn't enough. You need to learn how to speak to customers politely and reasonably. Most of us are not born even with these skills, to put it mildly. You also need to know how to *focus yourself and the caller on the task at hand, which is a brief conversation leading to a personal meeting.* Sales organizations are making a gross and obvious mistake when they do not use their best salespeople to answer phone enquiries. This first phone contact is a make or break point. Get it right and the customer will come and do business with you. Get it wrong and you have lost a sale and a customer.

You need to know how and what to say when answering a phone enquiry. You need to be ready with words and ideas that briefly explain why and how you can better help the customer face to face. This is more than just saying 'come in and see me.' This does not mean that you have a prepared script, but it does mean knowing the various ways you can communicate on the phone. You need to listen and answer questions in a manner that impresses the customer to come and see you in person. How you

THE AGREEMENT SUMMARY OF SELLING – A SERIES OF STEPS

do this will vary, but the key to it is to know what you will say next and how you will put it, otherwise it won't work.

There are days when we all do it just right, effortlessly and things just work out. Curious, huh? Yet, often selling on the phone is a chore and a pain. Usually we feel that way at those times when we are not doing it right. When you are doing it well, phone enquiries are easy and fun. So why not every time?

Here are some telephone techniques:

- Answer the phone quickly, by the 3rd ring. Even if you just tell the caller to hold on for a minute. But do not forget to come back to the call very quickly.
- Some companies have a prescribed way of answering the phone. This is not negotiable but watch your tone of voice.
- Ring customers back as soon as possible if you are too busy, but within one hour.
- Keep the calls as short as possible. Don't be impatient or too smart.
- Invite the customers to come in and meet with you personally.
- Your confident and assured behaviour will suggest knowledge, confidence and professionalism that will impress, inform and interest the customer.
- Suggesting that there are difficulties in giving service on the phone is fine depending on your tone of voice and the words you use. It is true that you cannot really offer proper service on the phone and yet most salespeople sound like they just want to get rid of the customer.
- Quote a price if they ask for one on a specific item, but if possible quote a price range. Keep the price details

loose. Customers rarely go to see a company who will not admit the price of an item.

- Tell the customer that you'd like to hear more about their needs and wants as there may be several other interesting new products and deals they may want to hear about. However, if you say this, make sure you know what you are talking about. Avoid getting caught up in a long conversation.
- Give them enough information to interest them. Be a person not a voice by projecting your personality.
- Get the customer's name so when they come in you might recall the phone conversation.

On the phone you mostly concentrate on researching and impressing the customer. It is good to briefly assure the customer with your company's documented guarantees, policies and advertised offers.

STEP 2 – RESEARCH YOUR CUSTOMER

There is nothing more important than finding out what the customer wants, or 'thinks' they need. "Oh yes, yes," I hear people saying already. "Of course, you have to find out what the customer wants." Most sales staff believe they are doing this by asking how they can help, and hearing a few words, they dash into demonstrating or offering a solution. This goes wrong all too often. You have to ask for more information to clarify your customer's wants. You and the customer must work as a team to solve the customer's problems.

Do your research and find out about:

- The customer

THE AGREEMENT SUMMARY OF SELLING – A SERIES OF STEPS

- The product
- The past relationship between your company and the customer
- The competition

Get this research step wrong or give the impression that you are not listening, or that you just want to get on with what you want to say, and you are sunk like the Titanic, never even knowing what iceberg you hit. Many customers are lost because the salesperson has not worked through the research phase. Proper communication will happen only if good research has been done.

Doing your research is the most important part of your presentation

- Ask how you can help and what the customer is interested in. Ask what results, that is, benefits/solutions, they want from this purchase. Make sure you get more than a simple one line answer, because what information you get now will tell you which way to head.

- Ask if the customer has purchased from your business before. This tells you about the relationship between your company and the customer. If they have purchased from your company before, they must have liked the experience to come back, so you are greeting an old and valued customer who, by the way, is likely ready to buy now!

- Find out what products your customer has seen already. This will give you clues regarding price range as well as many other facts such as whether they have been to a business competitor. It will also indicate what their product and feature preferences might be. Ask who will use the product and their expertise in dealing with the product. Ask what type and brand of products they have used before.

Like building anything, if you get the foundation wrong the whole structure will fall over.

STEP 3 – SET OBJECTIVES

**If you don't know where you are going
you are liable to end up nowhere…**

It is helpful to have an objective for each sale, but also always have a fallback position. Your main objective may be to sell a top range product; your secondary objective may be to sell a lesser product. If you can't get the sale now then your next best objective may be to make sure that the customer comes back. Life flies by quickly and your present actions are not a dress rehearsal. *There is no making up for the sales you did not get yesterday.* There is just what you do now. When you set sales objectives and go for them with purpose, gusto and commitment, you will know you did what you could in every sale. Even if you fail this time, you will have the good feeling that you gave it your best shot. This means working and living on 'purpose' and in control.

**Differentiate your company first, then
your product if possible**

In many small, large or even huge sales situations your competitors have similar or exactly the same products on offer and usually at very similar prices. So, why should people buy from you in particular? The following often used clichés will not convince customers: "we will look after you" or "we have the best deals" and the like. No point in saying these things unless they are true, AND you can prove it. Few customers will believe vague, generalized one-liners like 'we'll give you better service

THE AGREEMENT SUMMARY OF SELLING – A SERIES OF STEPS

than anyone else' unless you put what you offer into specific and definite forms.

> One way I differentiated my business from my competitors was to offer a 45 day unconditional exchange guarantee on hardware purchases to our customers at Ted's Camera Stores. This meant that a camera purchased from Ted's could be exchanged for any (or no reason) within a 45 day period, no questions asked, no money lost to the customer. This achieved exactly what I have just discussed. It demonstrated to the customer that we really offered a better service and were prepared to stand by it. Later on, Ted's Camera Stores improved on this concept by adding two other sensational guarantees. Usually if you buy a product and it happens to be faulty, (a lemon), during its warranty period, the manufacturer will fix it. Ted's found that faulty products, though few in numbers, tended to come back with further problems. The 'lemon' guarantee meant that if the camera purchased breaks down more than once during the warranty period, Ted's will replace it with a new one.
>
> P.S. All my competitors said that 'you can't do that'...so I knew I was onto something ...

Here is yet another sensational idea, even if I do say so myself. Ted's also guaranteed that customers could purchase whatever product they wanted at the best possible price. This 'Price Protection' policy was in print and made it immediately obvious to any customer that Ted's were serious about offering the best deals. All these guarantees were advertised and given in writing to customers. There may be other businesses offering great value and services but not many say so in no uncertain terms. (Please note that Ted's Camera Stores policies may have changed since the printing of this book.) In order for customers to buy from you, you need to differentiate your business from your competitors. Differentiate, prove it, and back it up. Being professionally different brings customer loyalty.

STEP 4 – SELLING BENEFITS: IS OFFERING SOLUTIONS

Really understanding this step can lead to awesome communication

No one buys anything but for what the product will do for them. Salespeople who are into talking about facts and features are telling, not selling – so I keep reminding the reader. People buy things because they expect some sort of benefit from their purchase. Let's look at the importance of features, and what exactly a feature is before we move on to what people actually buy.

Every benefit is provided by some kind of feature. The analogy of how our bodies work helps to explain this. Our individual body parts, organs, eyes, brain cells etc. have their own individual features which function to provide our bodies with benefits. Indeed, if a body part does not have the right features we get sick and the body does not work as well as it should.

Product features are always facts such as colour, size, shape, pattern and so on. Facts are not the same thing as explanations. We often mistake one for the other. Facts by themselves rarely explain themselves; they are just the facts. Your clear understanding of the difference between facts and explanations helps short-circuit communication breaks that easily happen otherwise. Facts are the features and properties of something.

THE AGREEMENT SUMMARY OF SELLING – A SERIES OF STEPS

The car is red and it is three meters long. These are facts. These facts do not explain or tell you what the car does. An explanation of what a product does could, sometimes, leave out just about all of the factual features.

We tend to call our explanations facts when trying to convince other people. This approach may create misunderstandings. Arguments may follow, and no one really wins an argument in a selling situation or in personal relationships. When we offer facts/features they are often not even understood by the customer. Even if they are, they may not show the customer why a particular product or model will be good for them or why they should purchase from you.

> Clear and suitable sales explanations tend to be about benefits and are extremely influential in convincing a buyer.

If you try and convince a customer to buy by using nothing but features and facts of a TV set or a car or a whole new piece of machinery, you are likely to fail. If you use only features when selling, all your selling will be about size, shape, colour, diodes, megabytes and lines per millimetre etc. all only descriptions. The customer, who may not understand all that, mostly will not admit they don't understand. Now just imagine you want to 'sell' me a relationship with you using only features. All you would be telling me is your height, age, and colour of your hair or perhaps about your last operation. That would be silly right?

If I do buy a product based on features it is because I am a professional or an enthusiast in a particular field and I know about the possible benefits of features. I have managed to imagine or understand the benefits the features will provide without your help.

SELLING IS NOT *JUST* TELLING

Every benefit of a product or service is driven by certain features and therefore by a certain purpose.

A benefit may or may not be readily obvious to many buyers. Furthermore, a benefit to me may be a drawback to you. The size of a small copying machine may not be a concern or benefit to me, unless I have limited space. To satisfy a want or a need is a huge part of successful selling. *Providing the right benefit to each customer* is the main thing that changes when you are selling. It is worth noting that a benefit to the customer always results in a benefit to the seller; a fixed tap for the plumber's customer, cured patients for the doctor, or a sale of products for salespeople are all benefits to both buyer and seller.

Here is an old story about benefits with a moral.

Two crows were lost in the desert for many days. They were desperately looking for something to eat and drink. "Well mate," said one crow. "This is it, I can't go on." The only thing near them in the middle of the sand was an old burnt out tree. "Wait, wait," said the other crow. "There's a tree. Perhaps we can find something under it." Weakly flapping their wings they headed toward the trunk of the tree. One crow sat at the bottom panting and exhausted, ready to die. The other with his last breath of energy flew up to the top. No sooner had he landed there than he yelled out, "Look at that, there is a cow paddy over there! Come on, let's eat that!" And he flew down and started to eat the cow dung. The other crow just watched him shaking his beak. He could not even think of it. His mate, now having filled his belly, started briskly flapping his wings breaking out into loud yells of 'ark, ark,' and then flew right up to the top of the tree. "Yippee and ark, ark!" he shouted, his eyes blazing bright. But suddenly there was silence and the crow dropped out of the tree, dead.

THE AGREEMENT SUMMARY OF SELLING – A SERIES OF STEPS

The other crow watched all this. Weak as he was, it still occurred to him that there was a great moral to the story:

Bullshit may take you to the top of the tree but it won't keep you there!

Explaining benefits properly results in a sale

You must explain what the product does and how that provides a benefit to the customer. Benefits are always the solution to the customer's problems. In fact, it is better to concentrate on the benefits first when demonstrating a product. For example, "This camera has a bigger zoom lens so you can get closer to the action and get more detail. That means you can actually see your son's face as he kicks that goal." At this point you can probably leave out how the camera does this. In any case, many customers have neither the expertise nor the interest in the mechanical features. In some situations, however, expert buyers may be vitally interested in features and facts.

If you haven't done a good job at the research stage, you are likely to flounder as the sale proceeds. You are likely to concentrate on nothing more than the product you are selling and that is not enough. If you did not ask the right research questions, if you did not build agreement so far, then it is at this point that the sale will most likely be lost. Often, a politely listening customer will sweetly smile, look at their watch and even break into your presentation to say something like, "Thanks for the information. I'll think about it...' If this happens, most likely you have lost the sale, as well as this customer, and you won't even know why.

Why? What happened? You probably moved into demonstrating a product, which was of little interest to the customer. You did not ask the right kinds of questions in the research stage. You did not found out what your customer expects as benefits from the purchase. It is possible, even likely, that the customer was not sure why or what they felt, except for one thing – they were not impressed enough with your presentation so far or they were actually put off, because you were not going where they wanted to go.

Let's rephrase this because it is so important. *Every time you hear 'bail out' words from a customer like, "Thanks very much, I'll think about it," you must acknowledge that something has gone wrong.* Quite right, chances are something has gone wrong. You have not held their interest or impressed them with your communication skills and not convinced them enough to listen any further. Boom, bang, crash, you've lost them. This happens to us all, and it is easy and sometimes even true to say, "Oh well you can't win them all." But take notice and ponder on what went wrong. Your mum or dad must have told you that making mistakes is okay as long as you learn from them. My experience tells me that most likely the research steps were not pursued well enough, and this being the case, you cannot move on to selling the right benefits to your customer.

Let's say that you have done your research properly and you are now doing 'show and sell' offering the customer actual products

THE AGREEMENT SUMMARY OF SELLING – A SERIES OF STEPS

or services. How you proceed from here is crucial. It is now that we separate the men from the boys, the girls from the women, the amateurs from the professionals. This is where the difference between 'telling' and 'selling' becomes vitally significant.

The point I am emphasizing and exploring is this *do not treat everyone as if they are robots wanting or needing the same benefits. Many do and many do not.* Often even the customers who are looking for a similar benefit might need to hear that benefit put in slightly different ways. Treat people as individuals. Oh yes, I know you know this already, and we all like to think that we are doing it. But I humbly suggest that you are not treating everyone as an individual. Without even being aware of it, we tend to treat women as women, guys as guys, oldies as such, yuppies as such, and all of them as 'customers.' This word 'customer' already has a connotation that they are all the same, so be aware of this in thought and in deed.

It is a strange affair, treating people as if they were all the same, since each of us want to be seen and perceived as an individual. Yet, we typecast people into groups, ages, gender, etc. *The customers must perceive that you see them as a person with unique needs.* If the dear customer does not get the feeling that they are a special individual who is heard and understood, "Well folks, it's all over red rover," as Robo, Managing Director of Ted's, used to put it.

> The real difference between amateurs and the successful sales professionals is that the professionals always repeat a successful strategy.

SELLING IS NOT *JUST* TELLING

The difference between features and benefits

Let's take a step back into this vitally important issue. See if you can answer these 'tricky' questions. Very few people have managed to do so in the hundreds of sales workshops in which I have used these silly but telling exercises. The answers are not as obvious as you'd think.

> **Question:** What is made in a shoe factory? Clue: Not shoes.
> **Question:** What's made in an iron foundry?
> **Question:** What's made by GMH or Ford?
> **Question:** Why do you want more money?
> **Question:** Why do we do anything at all?

Several answers are possible and some might be partly correct. But there is one correct answer that demonstrates the facts and what I mean. Before I give you the correct answer to the above questions consider another fun and silly story below. The story is about what real benefits are and it will provide you with some clues to answer the questions above.

Here is a tale of having to make a vital choice about what is a real benefit.

Imagine you've been shipwrecked. Luckily, you are just a couple of hundred meters from a beautiful uninhabited island with trees and a few monkeys, but nothing else. There are about ten of you swimming towards the island. The sun is shining, you can hear the birds singing and you are sure to get there. Still, the situation is a disaster. Just before your boat went down you were told that no other ships come near this island. The radio is gone there are no other means of communication. Your chances of getting picked up are nil. You will never be found. So let's face it, all ten of you may live, but you will have to be resourceful.

THE AGREEMENT SUMMARY OF SELLING – A SERIES OF STEPS

Gathering your senses as you swim toward the shore, you see some big barrels floating by, but they are floating away from the island. The barrels are marked. Quickly you all swim over to the barrels. There are two kinds of barrels. One barrel says it contains 'one million dollars' and the other says 'vegetable seeds, potato, beans, and apples.' Each of you can only grab one barrel. Which will you grab, the one with a million bucks or the one with the food and seeds?

In workshops where I have run this exercise we've had much fun discussing it. One or two people usually pick the million dollar barrel, thinking they will let the others do the work of seed planting and then buy the food. Others, more thoughtful, quickly see that it is never money we want, but always what the money buys, such as food and so on – the benefits. If, as is the case, money is useless on a deserted island and you will never be saved, why would you ever sell your potatoes?

So you see it is not money you want because it is worthless in itself, you can't eat it. You always want what the money might buy.

SELLING IS NOT *JUST* TELLING

People buy things for the benefit the product brings.

That's what my silly questions were about.

What's made in a shoe factory? The same thing as what is made in an iron foundry or in a department store: **MONEY**

Would anyone make shoes in a big way or invest in a business otherwise? Unlikely. All this points to the only thing people ever really want: benefits. You start a new business to sell cameras, make shoes or build houses. The actual benefit you are looking for is to make money. Not for the dollar notes as such, but for the benefit of what having money can bring to you. You invest in a particular business because you prefer selling cameras to selling salami. The benefit however, is the same. It is the making of an income, not sandwiches or keeping memories or becoming an artist. So, again: why do you go to work? To earn a living. Okay, but it is not for the plastic folded dollar notes, but for what the money you earn buys you!

Of course benefits are typically multi-levelled. One benefit is to the maker, several different ones to the customer. A shoe has many benefits – it protects your feet, makes you look better or helps you run faster. Benefits are rarely a one-line, one-off matter. You earn money so you can eat and live well, educate the kids, be creative, socialize and do something meaningful and satisfying.

There are usually several benefits to most products. A camera is bought for the pictures it takes, the memories. When you buy a car, do you do so because you love having two tons of molten plastic and metal in your front yard to look at? Perhaps you do. Then, that's a benefit. However, usually we buy a car for transport, safety, travel, fun, etc.

Do you want more money? Everyone says yes. Everyone wants more money, but recall the desert island story. There, potato seeds

THE AGREEMENT SUMMARY OF SELLING – A SERIES OF STEPS

were worth more than dollars. Some of the benefits of having money are that you can go on holidays, buy nice clothes, send the kids to school and so on. All these things have further benefits; a second line benefit such as holidays are restoring to you, or it is satisfying that your kids do well in life. Benefits are like ripples in a pond, *they seem to go on forever.*

Given that people only buy benefits it is strange that many businesses promote little more than the features of their products rather than the desirable benefits the product may bring to a buyer. On the other hand, a lot of businesses promote benefits very well only to find that their salespeople do not know how to sell those benefits.

What is a feature?

What is a benefit? Are they always the same? Or, are they always entirely different?

Do you need to discuss either if you think the customer is an expert in your product? It is always safer to point out benefits.

Unfortunately, a lot of features look like or sound like benefits to many salespeople who sometimes get hung up on beautiful features. *Such features may be excellent and well worth mentioning but never without the attached benefit!* Usually they are worth talking about to introduce what the particular feature does for this particular buyer. Get lost in talking about features and the customer's eyes glaze over if they are not interested in say, the latest advances in technology. In any case, many customers lost in technical jargon won't admit to it.

I am not as interested in the technical features of the new Kevlar sails for my boat unless you can tell me that this new Kevlar will give me a faster sail or easier handling. All I want is for the sail maker to tell me is that this new sail material is better because…On the other hand my brother, an engineer, wants to know the details about the Kevlar fabric and wants to know what testing has been carried out on its durability. A marine engineer is likely to be into features; he loves to know the details of new technology. Still, even for my brother, if you talk only features he may not understand why the Kevlar sail is any better than the product he currently uses. I am never impressed if the salesperson selling me a suit tells me about how the woollen material in the suit is so good the suit will last me for twenty years because I don't want to wear it for more than three years. I'm being offered a benefit that is of no interest to me. The salesperson must find out what I personally see as a desirable benefit of a particular feature. Human nature plays a large factor. People do not like admitting their ignorance. In retail particularly, few customers will challenge a salesperson that is just listing features. *Customers may not understand what benefit a feature* offers unless the explanation of the benefit is both clear and aimed at what *they wish to get from their purchase*. Another problem might be that customers hearing about fantastic features and technical details may think the product too complex, and possibly more fault-prone.

From features to benefits, an easy and natural move

When demonstrating products you need to have a 'transition line' that always takes you from talking about a feature to an attached benefit. A transition line is simply a bunch of words that take you from one idea to another. Here is a simple transition line: "This lens is a glass optic not plastic, which means that you get sharper pictures."

The transition line is: 'which means that'…

Simple, easy, problem free, just use it every time a feature is mentioned. It does not matter what transition line you use as

THE AGREEMENT SUMMARY OF SELLING – A SERIES OF STEPS

long as you always use one. This will make certain that each time you offer a feature a benefit is attached to it.

The tricky part is to clearly know what is a feature and what is the benefit of this feature, I repeat, for this particular customer. Every time you nominate a feature, you must follow this immediately by explaining what the benefit is. Then you must relate that benefit to this customer. For example, "You said that you are writing a book and you also want to use the computer to manage your business, so the larger and faster capacity of 1 terabyte will be important to you." Or, you might say something like this: "This computer has a nine gigabyte hard drive which means that it has the capacity to safely store all that you have typed. It will also be capable of storing accounting programs and even games and music...."

After stating features and benefits you must confirm that the customer understands, likes, and/or wants what you have offered. Use the summary agreement method. If the customer does not understand or want the benefits in the way you have presented them, you still have a chance to restate them in another way, or change track to another product. However, be careful that this does not make the customer feel put down. Miss this step and you may be missing the customer entirely. If the customer is in agreement then you have built an agreement summary. You are very close to finalizing the sale. Breeze over the confirmation part of an agreement summary too fast, and you are not building an agreement, you are back into telling rather than selling.

> What the product does or produces for the buyer is always the issue. There are no other issues.

Benefits are multi-levelled and they may be performance, appearance, comfort, safety, economy, fashion, emotions, profit, usually a mix of all those and then some. One of the main benefits of buying a camera is to record cherished memories of events. But there is more than just this; there are many other benefits. Some people buy the latest camera or car because they like to show off, or in order to exercise a creative impulse, or they just love the new glitter and technology.

It is not up to us to judge which benefits are more important, but it is up to us to find out which ones each customer sees as important.

A benefit is not necessarily obvious.

Let's say you are selling me a car. I have called into the showroom enquiring about a family car within a certain price range. The case is simple; you could never convince me about model 'X' being the fastest car in its class, or the least petrol thirsty, or that it has the largest capacity in its class. Why not? Several reasons are at play here. I may not care if any of the above is true. I may not have the expertise to understand why your statements may be true. Add to this the fact that high speed, petrol consumption etc. are not a major benefit for me. What is? That is what the salesperson must find out before offering me anything. The salient benefits for me may be safety, size and reliability.

If I answer your questions in very general terms, as customers often do, then you must find out enough about me (my personality type and my communication style) to appeal to the 'car buyer' within me. We will consider personality types and communication styles in some detail later in the book. I am saying again and again that you, salesperson, must find out what motivates and convinces me to buy a product. That means knowing what I, as the customer, think of as benefits.

People buy what they think things do for them both at a logical and at an emotional level. Everything depends on what a particular

THE AGREEMENT SUMMARY OF SELLING – A SERIES OF STEPS

customer sees as a benefit. Imagine you have done your research, demonstrated a product and explained the benefits as they applied to a particular customer. You've checked that the customer is in agreement; the product suits and appears to offer what they want. If you have sold benefits then agreement is likely to be forthcoming.

What next? You guessed it, I hope. Now that you have finished with your product demonstration it is time to do <u>summary listening again</u>.

Briefly summarize what you have shown and ask for confirmation that it is of interest. If you get confirmation regarding what has been discussed then perhaps it is time to close the sale. Perhaps, but not necessarily for the customer may have doubts, objections and concerns.

STEP 5. HANDLING OBJECTIONS

The customer's problems are your concern.

Whether the objections are correct, reasonable, realistic or not, if the customer has a problem you have to handle it. Most customers will raise some objections, which you need to handle before you can close a sale. Let's say that having done a professional job of your sales presentation you see that your customer still appears hesitant. If they voice their objections this gives you an opportunity to discuss their concerns. You cannot move on to finalizing the sale until agreement on a solution is reached. Perhaps the customer did not perceive that this product is the right product for them or they have some apprehension about the deal offered. An 'objection' is a concern a customer may have regarding your product or company, or about the offered deal.

Contrary to many ideas on selling, I believe *objections can be the best indicators that you might get the sale.* A customer's objection says simply this "I am not yet convinced, but I am interested enough to object." Then again, no objection from a customer might mean that they have no interest in your product or company or the deal offered. You will get no objections at all if the customer has missed your point, or more likely, you have missed what this particular customer is about. Objections may be:

- Hidden, perhaps even unknown to the customer; a kind of discomfort that means that s/he is not convinced.

- Exaggerated, perhaps in order to get a better deal.

- Truth bending by the customer, usually regarding the cost of your product. This is a sort of 'fishing' deal where the customer may try to see if a better deal may be arranged.

- Realistic concerns of a technical nature, which you have not answered. This is likely to do with your lack of confirmation that the benefits you offered are of interest to this customer.

- Actual and real problems the customer perceives. Possibly, you are trying to sell them the wrong product, usually because the research step was not well done. You have not found out what benefit they are looking for.

- Any other problem the customer sees, such as, delivery, paper work and so on.

THE AGREEMENT SUMMARY OF SELLING – A SERIES OF STEPS

Objections are usually a mix of all these and more. An objection always refers to perceived or not perceived features and benefits of the product or of your company.

Handling objections – not just 'answering' them but finding solutions.

There is something subtle here. 'Answering' an objection sounds, and usually is, defensive, and thus a reactive move from the seller.

'Handling' has a 'we are in this together' feel. The latter leaves out defensive feelings, punch-back and smarty comments. When we react to something it is invariably an automatic slap–back, usually without much thought and it moves us toward disagreement, argument and resentment. *Always start handling objections* with acknowledging and clarifying what the objection is. Then move on *using one of the various techniques outlined below*. This is similar to the summary idea we talked about at every stage of selling.

SELLING IS NOT *JUST* TELLING

Some customers may have real concerns about the product you have presented. These tend to be factual and refer to features. They may be worried about the weight of the caravan, fair enough, if they have only a small car. The cost of a product purchased as a present may also be a real objection. A camera that is too heavy is a real problem for a skydiver or for a back packer, but it may not be for others.

Often, customers who are unsure will use fudged or even untrue objections. These are due to the simple fact that they are not yet convinced. "I'll have to talk to the wife" can be one, but it may be true. "It has to be a blue one" may be a valid objection, but it isn't if there are no blue products made. "I'm not sure I need nine gigabytes" may be a real objection, but does it matter if all else is fine? So *consider whether the objection you are hearing is valid*.

Here are some of the simple ways to handle objections. They all have in common the idea that to satisfactorily handle an objection the seller must not create tension or dismiss the customer's worries.

- If you handle the problem from the customer's point of view you are on the right track. Neither a valid nor an invalid excuse coming from you will satisfy the customer if they have a problem.

- Excuses are out; understand and find a way to resolve the problem. Customers do not want to hear about your problems, they want to hear how you will resolve their objections.

- Anytime you say 'yes, but' you are not resolving the situation, you are just making things worse.

- *Use the 'side-stepping' technique to test if the objection is a real one.* This idea is best used for objections regarding features and cost. Simply put, you might confirm that: Aside from the weight, price or colour, does this machine seem to suit your needs?" Or, "Aside from the delivery (or whatever) do you think this product seems to be the answer to most of your needs?" Sidestepping gives you a bit of time out and also gives the customer a chance to see that there are many things they like about this item. Take care that it does not come out as a dismissal of the customer's worries.

- Never argue, challenge, or catch the customer out. We can get caught up in our own ego, particularly if we are not certain we have done a professional job. Even if you know a customer is not telling the truth about how they can get this item at a lesser price, what's the point of proving to them that you know they are lying?

- Do not counter-punch. The customer says he can get a bigger one, a smaller one, or a cheaper one and the salesperson says: 'May I ask you where?' Or even worse, 'No, that is not smaller it just looks like it is' and so on. Or even worse, 'If you can get one for less I'll have one too.' These are what we call a 'counterpunch' that clearly says to the customer 'I do not believe you, you are wrong and ignorant.'

- Do not get hooked. Easier said than done but...this means that you need to be aware of what pushes your ego buttons. Do not get hooked like a wriggling fish, don't get hooked emotionally or take what the customer says personally. If you get caught like a wriggling fish on a hook, your blood pressure rises, anger rises, confusion sets in and you lose your ability to think clearly. Many customers are expressing nothing more than 'I am not yet convinced' when objecting to your product. Sometimes they may not even be sure why they feel that way, so they find some objection to hang their hat on.

Handle situations carefully and calmly and try and get more details of the objection, rather than dismiss it or get caught up in it. If the objection is real and correct then simply admit that they are right about what they said and move on if possible.

- Re-state objections in positive terms where possible. Often this is easy, sometimes not. Let's say you are offering a low powered car. The objection is about the lack of power. A positive way of re-stating the benefit of this is to say that the driver is less likely to speed excessively and less likely to be booked for speeding.

- Offer compensating factors, if there are any. This is somewhat similar to the above example but you might suggest that money will be saved as a smaller engine uses less petrol.

- Put objections into perspective. Sometimes people get hungup on a small point. Everything seems fine but then they find out that the machine needs to be switched on two minutes before use. Be very careful when deciding whether it is a small point or not for this customer. It may seem small to you but big to them.

For example, I won't buy a car unless I get the colour I want, while others do not care about that. To put an objection into perspective reiterate the real benefits of the product and how they out weigh the one smaller problem. "We have agreed that such and such features and benefits will work well for you, is that right? There is a small draw back here; I can't supply a red one only a green one, but look at the many ways the product does suit what you need."

THE AGREEMENT SUMMARY OF SELLING – A SERIES OF STEPS

If the sale is stuck after you have addressed the objections, take a step back to the research phase or to selling benefits. Most of the time you will use a mixture of the above objection handling ideas. They are, after all, just good, clear methods of communicating. You know the old 'don't try this at home' warning? I suggest and recommend that you do try these techniques at home. Try it with friends and family; they are all experienced buyers after all.

Sometimes you can do a great job and handle all objections very well. For various reasons not every sale will happen at the time of the interview. Some sales cycles are short, as in retail, and some take months or years to finalize. Nevertheless, if you do it right then you have left the door open and the customer will be happy to return. In retail stores few people buy anything on their first visit, most will shop around. No matter what deals and benefits are offered elsewhere, most customers will come back to a store and salesperson that they like.

Bob Hawke used to say, "Arrggh, now having said that, let me say this," so now let me add this: If you handled the objections, but did not finalize the sale, then make sure that you have armed your customer with material so they can 'sell' for you at home or at their place of business.

STEP 6. CLOSE THE SALE NOW?

Maybe yes maybe no! Sale-closing ideas have been one of the greatest red herrings the oceans of salespeople have ever spawned. (A lovely metaphor, huh?) It is curious to note how reluctant salespeople are to ask for the sale. Why is that? Why does it seem such a big thing asking for a sale if you have done a good job of trying to satisfy your customer? One answer, I believe, is that you don't really feel that you have done such a good job. You know when it is easy to ask for the sale. It is usually when you have done it well and the customer is smiling at you and there is that warm fuzzy feeling. That warm and fuzzy feeling is just the situation you are building when you do things the right way.

Good research followed by selling features with attached benefits, asking good questions, checking by using summary with the customer that you are on the right track and handling objections which will be fewer if you progressed rightly than they would be otherwise. AT THE END OF THIS IT IS EASY TO ASK FOR THE SALE BECAUSE YOU KNOW YOU DESERVE IT.

Sometimes customers hesitate at the decision making stage because they feel that the deal you are offering is dubious. Perhaps they wonder if it is the best deal they can get. They can be reassured sometimes by a simple re-summary. Maybe a seller is reluctant to ask for the sale because he or she does not believe in the product being sold. That is a shame and ought not happen. Some people say a salesperson's reluctance is due to his or her feeling bad about a possible 'knock-back.' No one likes a 'knock-back,' but I suggest that the feeling of being rejected is only true if you have not done a proper job of the sales interview.

If all went well you will feel the kind of confidence that comes with knowing you have done your best. We've all experienced this 'warm fuzzy' feeling when we achieved something. The achievement does not need to be a world record. You may lose a game of tennis, but look how different you feel when you have done your best as opposed to an off day when you know you did not.

There has been a lot of nonsense written about sale closing.

There are books and workshops on closing the sale, offering various torturous schemes, weird questions and methods, none of which have ever worked for sellers or buyers. There is no mystery to

THE AGREEMENT SUMMARY OF SELLING – A SERIES OF STEPS

closing the sale. All it really means is ending the sale presentation by asking the customer to buy. You can do that by *offering a solution*, or by *suggesting a decision or by asking in any way you like*. The only point is that you must ask. Providing your presentation was good and agreement has been built, you can ask decently and definitely because you have earned the sale. Things go wrong when you ask after a poor demonstration or when you ask at the wrong time.

Closing the sale starts with looking for 'ready to buy' signals

What is a 'buying signal'? There are lots and lots of them. In a retail situation the customer may be looking for their credit card … or asking their partner what they think…or asking whether this product is available in a different colour, size, quantity…or at a better price. All of these are buying signals. Do not mistake them for anything else.

In a longer sales cycle situation the customer might ask for possible delivery dates and situations or payment terms…or guarantee details…or better price terms. All these are, or might be, buying signals, not problem signals. It means you are now only negotiating about the price or the details of the contract. Your presentation has been accepted.

Now you have arrived at closing the sale. You are hearing 'buying signals' and it feels right. This is the time you might ask closed questions since those questions need a decision, a yes or a no, by any other word. In an effort to take the fear out of sale closing, think of this sales step simply as making an offer or proposing a decision.

Asking for the sale can and should be simple and easy. Perhaps you might ask, "Which product is more attractive?" If they pick one, ask, "Should we settle for that then?" Or you can simply make an offer as follows: "How do you feel about using this one?" If the answer is positive your next question is the old, "Will you eat it here or take it away?" Ha Ha. If you have what appears to be agreement then do not muck about, ask for the sale. No one likes 'pushy' but if you do not ask for a buying decision then some sales will simply fade away from you. Customers sometimes need help to make a decision. How many times should you try to close the sale? Twice I think, but neither times in a pushy way. Your first try follows your demo stage and summary, assuming that buying signals are present. If the customer does not say yes then summarize again and look for a buying signal: "Do you have any preference?" or "How does this deal sound?" If you get a positive answer ask for the sale again. If not then you may need to let it go for now.

If a customer has left the store or you have left their office after a polite refusal, it pays to ask yourself what happened. It pays well to do this even when you have made a sale. *Don't just see what went wrong, consider and 'bed-in' what went right. Put open questions to yourself and think about what you did.*

Don't throw away your own questions with the usual excuses used by salespeople like 'he was not ready to buy' or 'he is still shopping around'...or 'he does not have the dollars to spend.' All these may well be the case, but you know if you have paid proper attention to the customer, whether what you were told is likely to be fair dinkum (truth/correct) or not.

If you have done your job well it is most likely this customer will call upon you later. If you doubt that, if you have not gained the confidence that a proper interview would have given, then you might not hear from that customer again. Yes, it is also true that no matter what we do or how well we do it, we cannot win them all. However, we can certainly up the odds in our favour.

No one wants a weak leader.

THE AGREEMENT SUMMARY OF SELLING – A SERIES OF STEPS

As a salesperson, you need to remember that customers ask for your advice or opinion because they want to hear what you, the expert, recommends. Clients need salespeople who demonstrate expertise and can confidently guide them toward a good solution. People want a confident salesperson who has an opinion and will help them to make a decision.

Salespeople often think that they are asking for a sale by saying something like, "Either of these three cameras will do what you want." Well, no, although this way of doing it is not a total disaster, it is of no actual help to your customer either. Nor does it call for a decision. It is better and preferable for you to say something like this: "From what we have discussed I think brand X will suit you best. What do you think?" The customer will either agree or hesitate and look at the other brand. If they agree, get your invoice book and start writing or ask for the sale. If they hesitate you might head towards the other product because presumably all of the products you have shown are suitable anyway. The customer can be genuinely conflicted about which product to choose or which store or business to buy from. It is up to you to show leadership.

In the end, if the customer has not dismissed you, is still there but hesitant, this is a strong buying signal telling you that you simply must do something. So ask, beg but do something. However, do not say this "Perhaps you'd like to think about it a bit more?" Oh dear me! This may sound all right, but it is a disaster, for you are actually telling the customer, who is still engaged in the buying process, to go away. This is rather silly and shows that the seller simply does not know what else to say.

In any case remember that pushy selling is out. The moment the customer feels pressed you have lost not just this sale, but also the customer. If you get pushy, or if you have gone too far, or if you have genuinely done all you can then all that is left to do is to give up, as John Cleese suggested. Cleese, the great comedian from the TV series Faulty Towers, has made a whole series of brilliant sales training films. In one of these films, Cleese, always the 'faulty' salesman, said something that is not just funny but also true. In one particular scene he tried his best to sell to his customer and apparently failed. He was asked if he knew what to do now that he had tried all he knew. With a look only Cleese can give he said, "I'm gonna go and look for a good tandoori chicken for lunch. I deserve it."

> I have a confession: Many times, having arrived at the point of asking for the sale, I actually did say, "It appears that we have found what you are looking for. And if we have, will you eat it here or take it away?" To my customers this seemed funny. What it did was to break the sale closing/decision making ice, if there was any left to break, and it brought a smile and the nod. "Yes we'll take it."

CHAPTER 5

ADD ON SELLING IS ADVANCED SELLING AND SERVICE

Selling accessories to customers is good customer service. Let's say you have made a sale, now is the best, and perhaps the only time, to sell more. This is easy to do. However, before you think 'ah, greedy' perhaps we should change the title of this section to *'Enhancing the purchase for the buyer by offering more information* – while making more money for your company and yourself. This is a true win/win possibility if you are genuine and well prepared. This sounds much better, and it is no sleight of hand because this is exactly what you will be doing for the customer. Offering accessories is useful to the customer. Accessories will enhance the value and benefit of the product they have purchased.

SELLING ACCESSORIES AND EXTRAS

You are doing customers a disservice when you do not suggest or inform them about accessories for the purchased product. Many customers are likely to need some accessories, spares, materials and so on. Usually they will buy these, sooner or later, from a competitor's store if you don't let them know what is available at this time.

For example, the computer and printer buyer who lives in the suburbs, but purchased in the city, will not come back to the city for spare paper or cartridge supplies or for the dust cover for the monitor. I bought a car in the suburbs, but bought all my accessories for it from my local dealer in the city. It is not just retail items we are talking about but all selling situations.

Some salespeople feel a bit shy about add on sales, but re frame it to what it is. All you are doing is *offering items that enhance the original purchase*. This is not greedy, it really is customer service. All you do once the main sale is concluded is to inform and suggest accessories or additional items by explaining (as usual) the *benefits of the accessories*.

Either you know what the benefits of those accessories and additional products are, or you do not. There is no half way here either. The benefits must be put, as usual, from the customer's point of view and must be of some apparent benefit to them. Car dealers are good at this – sort of. But oh, in what a strange way do they do this add on selling. Some dealers employ a special sales person to do the selling of additional items, rather than the person you have just bought the car from. As it happens, most of these accessory salespeople are badly trained and in my opinion their companies are making a mistake. The 'special' accessory salesperson knows nothing about this customer, as they were not included in the initial sale of the car. How could the special salesperson know what the customer might like, or want, or consider a benefit? Sometimes they are downright pushy and just rattle off the extras. How could they offer benefits tailored to the particular buyer, when they have not heard much from

ADD ON SELLING IS ADVANCED SELLING AND SERVICE

him/her? Lucky for them and their companies, most people love gadgets and extras and will usually buy some of them.

Here is some of what you must not do! Imagine the customer said 'yes' to the product you've been discussing. As you reach for your invoice book, you start suggesting extra items, sort of rattling them off. Hello, hello, you are right if you feel a touch uncomfortable about this. To some customers it will seem like you are getting greedy, wanting more money from them. *The proper way to sell accessories and extras is to discuss them during the actual sale of the main product.* Professional sellers inform and educate the buyer throughout the product presentation about accessories that will enhance the purchase. Clients want to know what is available. The buying decision is left to the customer. Ah, friends, but this means you have to truly know what you are going to say and when you will say it. Preparation is necessary and it will easily pay for your extra work.

What extra items you should or can offer will come out of your communication with your customer as a natural progression. Right through the presentation, you will hear about what benefits the customer expects. Remember we said earlier that everyone buys benefits; accessories and extras provide and can extend those benefits. This is another reason why the early step of researching the customer's ideas, needs and wants is so important. My research shows that clients who are offered extras are never offended if this *offering* is done properly. They like to hear about what an intended purchase is capable of doing, even if they are not interested in purchasing at that particular time.

> All you need to do is to 'mention' the extras in your presentation, at the appropriate moment, always attaching the benefits these items may bring.

Some examples:

- A tow bar is good for towing, but it also keeps other cars from bumping into you, and carries the bike rack (you already know there are children and weekend outings). Or you know there are bumps on the trade in...or...)

- A polarizing filter for the camera is like 'sunglasses for the camera' – it will ensure your pictures are sharper and brighter instead of appearing washed out (everyone takes pictures in bright sun or snow etc.)

- An ergonomic keyboard may not be necessary but in the long run it will provide you with more comfort and less chance of repetitive strain injury.

- The more powerful modem will ensure better wireless connection (perhaps you know the client lives in a multistorey home).

- Now that you have engaged our monthly services perhaps you might like to know more about our holiday plan?

No? They are shaking their heads, fine leave it. But if you try for that extra add-on sale every time then you are likely to be a far better sales person and earn more money into the bargain.

Inform the customer about various accessories throughout the sale as potential benefits. At the end of the sale you simply remind them – by way of asking a simple question – "So can you see the tripod might be useful?" Or "Does the spare battery seem like a good idea?" or "What do you think of the extra guarantee and the super polish package?" This is another version of summary agreement selling and it is likely to result in the customer choosing some of the extra products you have offered.

> Great customer service is effortless; doing the thing right is the same as doing the right thing.

NEGOTIATING A MARGINALLY PROFITABLE DEAL

Negotiating is the art of bringing something to a closure in such a way that it suits both parties. Industrial or large sales negotiating can be very complex, a separate art and technique and I leave that subject to others for the time being. There is however, one easy and simple idea to keep in mind about negotiating. This idea incorporates just about all other ideas on negotiating. Put simply and bluntly, *"If I give you this, what do I get?"*

Of course, you do not put it quiet like this. How you say it will depend on what you are selling and to whom. However, 'If I give you this, what do I get?' is what it all boils down to whether it is about a political conflict, or about the sale of a camera, or a fleet of cars, that's the bottom line. If I must give away more than what I want to, then I must get something in return.

If you must cut your price below what your company considers profitable, then perhaps the sale is not worth making. This may be so, but it is short sighted if you let it go at that. Better to try and make some add-on sales to help 'cushion' the profit margin. The fact is that in many areas of selling, accessories bring a better profit margin than the hardware does. *The customer will buy a product from someone.* You have done the work, surely it is better to negotiate and accept a reasonable profit than do nothing at all. What is 'reasonable' is something that will give each side some of what they want, even if it is not all that they hoped for. Most customers are reasonable enough providing they are *well treated and impressed* by the salesperson's presentation. You can't win them all, but you can win a lot of them if you do it right.

INTERNET ON LINE SALES AND HOW TO HANDLE THEM. PRICING PROBLEMS.

Almost any business has problems with pricing and the deals they offer. Buyers will naturally look for the best possible deals. This is true whether a buyer is looking for a low cost mobile phone or a plant of machinery. What tends to go wrong when finalizing a deal is that most salespeople do not know how to handle the pricing issue as well as they should.

ADD ON SELLING IS ADVANCED SELLING AND SERVICE

At this point I must mention the rising problem of on line Internet sales particularly, (but not only) for retailers. It is interesting to note that many retailers also sell on line, often offering the same products at a lesser price. The whole thing is in some murky flux that, I believe, will settle somewhat in time. Meanwhile hands on salespeople have a problem of often having to match low prices to that of an Internet site that works without a shop front, rental and sales costs for staff. Worse, a lot of customers will come in to stores, get the information and then shop on the net.

Sales marketing has not caught up with this phenomenon as yet. I know of no store that has adequately and actively pointed out the benefits of buying from them as compared to buying from a faceless web site, many of which come and go.

> If you do not have anything to offer that is better and is beyond what a web site offers then you better work on that problem.

I have purchased something on line from a well-known internet store and find I cannot take it back to an actual store (it is in the US) to get it fixed under guarantee. I need to pack it up and send it…I have also changed my mind about the product etc. etc…

I believe that stores could and should point out to clients that they are not a public service, and that they do offer more than a web site. This has to be done specifically; specific offers and features need to be built. Many years ago at Ted's we had the almost same problem with duty free stores in Australia, and even more so overseas. It was very frustrating to serve a customer well only to have him say how impressed he was, and then to say that he will buy this camera from Singapore or New York. My solution to that problem was and is similar to what's happening today, although today is a little harder to tackle. At the time Ted's offered customers a try before you fly deal. That allowed them to make sure the camera they bought from us was working well, and that it was the right model for them. We offered an unconditional exchange, and some extra education (after hours) on picture taking. This greatly improved our situation, but eventually we opened a duty free store of our own. So then we were in competition with all the faceless overseas stores. It was not hard to beat those. And it was a big step for Ted's.

The point is that particularly, but not only, retailers, must come up with reasons why the customer should buy from them. Retailers must get together and actively promote such features that show why it is better to buy from a store. Sales staff need retraining in how best to sell both their own company and the goods they offer.

> BEWARE! The first and biggest issue now is selling your company's store; selling the product or a service has become the secondary issue!
>
> (This was always true, but now it is even more important.)

There are a number of things retailers can do to combat on line sales from overseas. I will now be bold enough to suggest some of the most obvious:

- Form associations to brainstorm and action good ideas and then market them as a body of retailers in each section of retail and also together as retailers of Australia (or whichever country you are in). The same goes for some manufacturers and service providers. Your main competitors are not the people in another store selling the same things. Your biggest competitors are the Internet on line sellers in other countries.

ADD ON SELLING IS ADVANCED SELLING AND SERVICE

- Lobby the government to charge GST (tax) on goods purchased on the net. Do not believe that it is too hard to do that!

- There are no guarantees on many of products if purchased from online stores in other countries; this is the case with several big camera brands for example. Make sure customers know these things. Display the story, re-train the staff.

- It is easy to say that if the dress does not fit so well you can fix it or that you can always send things back for a refund but we all know that all these sorts of things are a pain to actually do.

- Do point out to customers the importance of buying locally, but do it right; know what to say that might influence people.

- Lobby your suppliers for exclusive brands not available on the net. Yes it can be done, to a degree at least.

- DO NOT buy goods from suppliers who blatantly charge too much in Australia (or where you live) to retail stores. What is the point anyway?

- Display mainly products that are less likely to be sold on the net.

- Do not rubbish brands or suppliers; that is pointless. But if you know that there have been many complaints against XYZ on line stores in England or in Baluchistan, then use that, and prove it, carefully.

I reiterate that staff must be re trained and supplied with issues and guarantees or services that effectively fight on line buying.

Australian retailers and sales organizations really must get together and act in their own interest.

Change is always hard, but businesses make it harder than it needs to be by taking too long to see the changes and by being unimaginative about what they can do about it all. It is possible that businesses need to make and take big steps; stop selling some brands or buying from better sources overseas. The publishing industry, for example, is still living in the past, holding on to their beloved paper books, but even they are beginning to look at what is obvious – Ebooks.

It would be presumptuous and silly for me to try to offer more actual advice on where and what a business should do. Only the management and staff in each retail specialty area can help with input on change. Do involve your sales staff in improving this problem.

Clearly, what sort of world will we have if there are no stores and people we can buy from eye to eye? Surely price is not everything, and that has been proven time and again.

"Is that your best deal?"

Back now to the usual often heard pricing problems in almost any sales presentation. A great deal of nonsense is sometimes put forward by salespeople when a potential buyer asks for a 'better' deal. Proper handling of the situation will greatly help to finalize the sale for both parties. There are a number of suggestions I would like to make.

First, get rid of the whole idea that price problems are an actual problem. Rather, view it as what it is, a 'buying signal.' So far in this sale you have done well, don't lose it now. The customer wants your product. That is the first hurdle. Price is important but a secondary point. There is a famous story about G. B. Shaw

ADD ON SELLING IS ADVANCED SELLING AND SERVICE

the English writer, who at a dinner party was seated next to a fine looking woman who was, unfortunately, also very boring. Exasperated, Shaw turned to her at one point and asked whether she would consider making love with him for a million pounds. After much merriment around the table, she agreed. Shaw then asked, "Well, how about for only 100 000 pounds?" There was much laughter by all present and the woman after some thought, agreed to this sum also. After all, this was a huge amount of money back in those days. Without any hesitation Shaw then offered 100 pounds for lovemaking! Her eyes sparkled with anger now. "Certainly not sir, what do you take me for?" Shaw answered thus, "Madam we have already established that...we are only haggling about the price."

> The point is to understand that if we are haggling about price the sale is almost made! You might lose it now if you do it wrong.

Yes, there will be times when you cannot meet an unreasonable demand but it is likely that no competitor can either. Here are some things to keep in mind regarding pricing issues:

- Make sure when the price seems a problem that it actually is the real buying issue. Customers often ask for a lower price as a matter of habit. Ascertain whether it's your price that is too high or the cost is above what the client wanted to spend. These are two entirely different issues. Test this by offering another lower priced product if possible to clarify the situation. Sometimes this side stepping technique works and helps the customer as well.

- Ensure that a price comparison between your product and the opposition's is 'apples against apples.' Take care, do not 'catch them out' and don't embarrass the customer.

- Make sure your quote is competitive and yet profitable, but even more importantly, that *your quote includes other good reasons* as to why the customer should buy from you. These can be things such as your guarantees or fast repair service, but remember you need serious and provable service offers, not the usual 'she'll be right, we look after you, mate' nonsense.

- Do not get frustrated if the customer tells you that they have a better offer. Do your concerned face! But do not get emotionally hooked, counter punch or catch them out so the customer 'loses face.' Customers can make honest mistakes and/or quote a lower price from a competitor than you offered. Sometimes there is not much you can do about that other than doing a good job of the selling steps. Leave the door 'open' so the customer can come back to you.

- Do not offer lame duck unbelievable excuses, lies, or silly suggestions as to why your price is higher. These are all what I term 'bunkum.' No one will believe you and most will feel offended.

There may be times when you simply must match a lower price in order to make the sale. Company policy will play a part in this, but here is the proper technique. Selling has a little bit of 'theatre' about it. A restaurant is a theatre, so is a camera store or a car yard or a real estate agent etc. Business people dealing with the public present a certain face, both in the way they look and in the way they promote themselves. This is most obvious in the retail business. Some stores look posh and expensive while others look more like a warehouse. There is an amount of showmanship

ADD ON SELLING IS ADVANCED SELLING AND SERVICE

in the way a business is conducted and marketed. The following presents using an element of 'theatre' when dealing with the customer who will buy *if you offer them a better price...*

Many customers will ask 'Is that your best price?' This often means only what it says. On hearing this question salespeople often think that they have to go to a lower price. Perhaps so, but maybe not.

When asked for a better price, or a price match, always call 'another' into the conversation – the manager if possible, or another salesperson. If you can and must reduce price, then first get your associate, the 'other' to *confirm with the customer that they are ready to buy*. This means that you and your associates must have your 'act' together. Everyone must know how to handle such situations. The 'other' confirms with the customer that this product is what they want. If the customer agrees, the lower price is agreed to, after the 'other' and you study your price list. To complete the act, always use your calculator and take a few seconds to deliberate. Only then you agree to, or offer a lower price.

Why do we use the 'other'? Why not just do it by yourself? For one thing, calling in another person confirms that you care and want this sale. It shows the customer that you are concerned and even if nothing can be done about lowering your price *you retain your relationship with this customer*. Your helper should refuse the price reduction (if that is what you need to do). The customer will see that you have tried to improve the deal; you are on their side. The 'other' can be a bit firmer when asking the customer for commitment. For instance your colleague might ask: "If we match that price will you be buying the product now?" If the customer says yes, the sale is made. If they do not commit, then it might be better to leave the door open inviting them to check with you when they are ready to purchase. CAUTION: Be careful, do not be smart, rude, tough, etc. Do it with a smile. You have built a relationship so far, don't wreck it now. Note that calling in someone else also makes it 'safer' for you when the bean counters want to know who authorized a sale at a lesser margin.

What if you cannot call in someone else? Consult the price list anyway, use your calculator and ask the customer if this is what they want and if they are ready to buy. If they are not ready to buy do not be too cagey. You can do something terrific here. Still match or confirm or lower the price and then tell them that they will have to *check again when they are ready to buy because prices do go up and down.* (Currency rising etc.)

I said that 'prices could go up and down!' Note up and down, not just up. I said that 'prices could go up and down!' Note up and down, not just up. I said that 'prices could go up and down!' Note up and down, not just up.

The point is to dangle the carrot in an effort to get the customer to re visit you later, if the sale cannot be finalized now. It is often true that prices go down for various reasons, yet salespeople always seem to opt for the hard to believe scenario that prices may go up. Why would you go back to a business if you have been told prices might go up? But if prices might go down by the time a customer decides to buy, it is worth their while checking with you. You get another chance, providing the buyer was impressed. This is subtle, radical and true anyway.

Some people object that the above is virtually saying to the customer that you may well have a better deal later on. Well, you do not have one right now, and may never have one. All you said was that you do not know if price or availability etc. will improve or get worse. The difference is that you are actually offering something potentially positive rather than only negative.

SELLING DOWN, NOT UP. A VERY SPECIAL SALES TECHNIQUE.

Think about this, it is radical. Every customer has had the experience when inquiring about a product, that the salesperson's first question was about their budget. This is a very bad start. After all, it is a product we are selling not dollars. Let's say the customer offered to nominate a price. Often, salespeople proceed to show a more expensive price range than was nominated. Really bad again. Many salespeople seem to have the idea that they must always try and get as much as they can when in fact, they should first try to secure a sale and a customer. Distrust is likely to arise if the customer perceives that a salesperson is trying to dig into their pocket. Particularly if the seller has not bothered to find out what the customer really wants or actually needs.

All these salespeople are doing is talking price, dollars not products, dollars not benefits. If the seller bothers to justify the higher priced item they usually do so only with *inane feature rattling – telling not selling.* Typically they suggest nothing more than that the dearer product is better than the lower priced one because of the higher price. Hmm and aha, is what I think when I am the buyer, but rarely say so. These sellers have lost me, and will lose many potential customers unless they explain in customer centred terms the benefit of spending more money. It would be far better to forget price at the beginning of any sales presentation. Certainly, one needs to establish sooner or later the customer's possible price range. *The answer to the price range question usually crops up by itself* from your good research questions.

SELLING DOWN, NOT UP WORKS

My suggestions about selling 'down' rather than up work well on every occasion, unless you commit the sin of not properly listening to the customer. In my businesses, my staff and I used this technique and it helped to make not just sales, but many extra satisfied customers. We all felt genuine in our selling endeavours, and that was also helpful to morale. These are productive ideas for any sort of selling or negotiating. Before I explain further how to do it correctly, I want to be certain it is understood that whether you are selling 'down' or 'up' you need to be genuine and will have to prove that what you offer is the right product for this specific customer.

Asking what the customer has in mind to spend at the start of a sale is not necessary in any case. Experienced sellers will recognize some of the following:

- The customer will not necessarily tell you the truth about how much they wish to spend. Unfortunately, this is because they do not trust salespeople. Or the customer may not be clear on how much they need to spend to get what they want, (often the case when I am buying.)

Let us say that you are at the stage of the sale where you are summarizing what you heard from the customer and what you think they want or need. Now you nominate an approximate price range, asking for confirmation from the customer that you are in the right ballpark. For example, 'From what you told me, I think we may be looking at a Canon X or a Pentax Y model with a 3 times zoom. These are in the $300-$500 price range. How does that sound to you?'

The customer will either consent that this price range is appropriate, or say something like, '$500 is too much, I did not want to go over $400. Some people may also indicate that $500 is okay, and they may even go a touch higher if etc…This is all you need to know for now.

ADD ON SELLING IS ADVANCED SELLING AND SERVICE

Now we are at the stage where selling 'down' rather than up, kicks in. Let's assume either the previous scenario or that the customer has come to you and told you up-front their price limit is up to $1000. In any case, you have found out that the $1000 price range suits. You proceed now by showing them two different products. *Perhaps one about $900 and another just over $900, but both under the limit of $1000.* Tell the customer (only if it's true) that either of these may be all they need as they have all the benefits that the customer wants.

Nothing is wrong with this so far as long as your suggestion is genuine and the products will, in fact, do the job requested. *Already your credibility will have risen in the customer's eyes.* That credibility and confidence in you is like gold; it is good for both the seller and for the customer. However, this will happen only *if the customer feels you have researched their needs*. You are showing your customer goods, not above, but below their agreed price range. Well, well, well. Suddenly you are no longer the 'shark' every customer tends to expect every salesperson to be. You are building credibility and trust.

So far you have told the customer why and how the $900 item will meet their needs. Then tell them, (only if it is true) why the $960 item might be better. Now you might also mention why one over $1000 may be even better, (if that is the case) and you can demonstrate or prove that to be so. What you have done so far is to demonstrate your genuine interest in satisfying the customer's needs by offering proper choices.

Some sales managers may object to what I just suggested. After all, they argue, it is better for the business to sell as many higher priced items as it can. True enough, but possibly short sighted. If the customer buys the $900 camera *they will show and tell others about the great buying experience* they have had, and about the genuine seller they purchased from. Even better, as a rule they will spend some extra money on accessories and become a regular customer of that business; that business can be trusted. It is a fact of commercial life that margins tend to be lower on hardware than on accessories. Therefore, if I sell a $1000 product my margin may be less than if I sell a $900 product plus $100 worth of accessories.

If you have found that what the customer wants cannot be purchased for the $1000 they were prepared to spend, you cannot sell down. Honesty and good ethics will not allow it and a sale will not result if you try to do it.[1]

Many pricing problems and cutting your profit margin may be avoided when you are asking the customer to spend less than what they had in mind.

---

1   Ever since I started it in 1970 and until the day I sold it in 1986, Ted's Camera Store was operated on these principles and it worked very well for the company and for the customers. The point was always that I'd rather have a $900 sale than none.

ADD ON SELLING IS ADVANCED SELLING AND SERVICE

Now let's take the case of a customer who comes to you asking for a specific brand and model of product. Proceed as follows. Let's say the customer has asked for a Smartgrape computer No 350 with X amount of memory and is prepared to spend up to $3000. Here is what you know when you have heard this: Clearly they have done some homework and have established what they need. If possible, you might still offer a lower priced product – if that product satisfies all their needs. Take care though; some people have their minds made up on a particular model and brand. Even then, offering a lower priced product still shows that you are not a shark looking to bite them as hard as you can. Thus you have established more credibility than you would have otherwise.

Some customers prefer prestige products. If the customer wants a prestige product like a Mercedes car you do not try to sell them a Holden. Precisely because part of the benefit this customer is looking for is the prestige and quality a Mercedes brings them. Customers do not always know or tell salespeople what they prefer or why that is the case. It is up to us to discover that. It is impossible to tell by the appearance of the customer what they might wish to spend on a product. Many salespeople have taken a look at me in my old jeans and t-shirt and have decided that I would only buy a cheap second hand sailboard. I had to tell them what I wanted in a sailboard, they did not ask. Then, I had to say that I did not mind spending more than the price range they nominated. One silly fellow then told me that I did not have to spend more! Fine, at least I did not feel like he was a shark but what was he playing at? The real issue is to find out the benefit any particular customer is looking for. It is never the salesperson's responsibility to decide what a customer wishes to spend.

To keep selling 'down' or to offer a lower priced product once the customer has told you otherwise is emphatically not what I suggest. Doing so is simply not listening to the customer at all. Look at my case with the sailboard. There were several practical reasons why I was willing to spend more on a sailboard. The salesperson never found out what these were. Because I am not a young fellow, I find it difficult to water start a sailboard once I have fallen off, and that happens a lot. Therefore I need a large stable sailboard so I can easily climb back up on board. I also wanted one of the new lightweight ones that I knew cost more. It is unproductive for both the customer and your business to do what the sailboard seller did to me. You are not there to decide what the buyer's heart and pocket may decide. But you are there to get answers to those sorts of questions. *As a professional you are someone who 'professionally helps the customer get what they want.' The emphasis is on help and choice.* Getting the customer's confidence eventuates in a sale, but you must be fair dinkum.

In summary, always start with sufficient research, followed by a demonstration of the features and benefits specific to your customer's needs within the required price range. Be real, be honest and be attentive to the responses you get. Involve the customer by summary listening and good questioning. Confirm your discussions throughout the sale. Whether you are asking the customer to spend more or less you must concentrate on benefits. Benefits can be many faceted or just one.

So, what were they really looking for as benefits? Ah, as that well-known English salesman of words, William Shakespeare was fond of saying, 'That is the question.'

'ACTION STATIONS'

It should be company policy to make absolutely certain that all the information and things you need to make a sale are at hand. Price lists, comparisons, results, news items, delivery dates, products to demonstrate, calculator, etc. etc. should all be at hand or in your brief case. Professionals do not fumble for anything. In a retail

ADD ON SELLING IS ADVANCED SELLING AND SERVICE

situation, you need to set up several 'action stations' through the store because these will help you sell. If you are a company representative, the same thing applies to the inside of your brief case or your laptop. Many sales are lost, or take twice the time, due to things not being at hand. It may be information, samples, documented results and so on. Action stations are needed at each major hardware or service point in retail not just at one but at several places.

In a camera store for example, the action station will have the examples of pictures you get from the camera you are offering. In a car showroom there will be leaflets, comparisons, tests, and so on. In other areas of sales, you might have testimonials from happy customers, comparisons with your products and the competition's products. There is rarely a case where you cannot actually and readily show or demonstrate some of the desirable benefits and results your product brings.

A PHOTO ALBUM OR AN IPAD

'A picture tells a thousand words.' Most of you probably do not sell cameras, but stick with me and see how you might apply the following in principle in your sales area. It is a laughable fact that in all my years in camera retailing very few salespeople everused a photo album of samples. We had to push and prod to get the sales staff in a camera store to use their own pictures to sell cameras. I wondered what was going on there. Finally, we made up several albums showing the results of our favourite cameras, the ones we preferred to sell. The pictures showed what the zoom lens, red eye correction, auto flash etc. did. The pictures were taken by us and showed each of us in the store or at a social function. Customers could relate to the pictures because we could actually point at the people shown in the photo. This made the photos credible to the customer as opposed to the lovely glossy pics taken by some pro of Elle McPherson or a famous racing car driver.

The above is just one example, but *the photo album/tablet can be used whether you are selling fish, cars, computers or industrial machinery.* Keep in mind that *it is the benefits, you show in the photographs not just the product.* What you show in the pictures should be outcomes, 'benefits' but not supercilious pictures. For example, a few shots of a bush scene you took when you went there in the 4-wheel drive you are selling ought to show your face to give it credibility.

Or show the internals of the gearbox and how they are still in good nick after five years. The album might also have testimonials from satisfied customers, comparison tests and so on. Even an explanation of how your guarantees work or how fast your servicing department operates, all these type of things help.

GETTING MORE UNDECIDED CUSTOMERS TO RETURN

Many people do not make a buying decision on the spot, particularly if you are their first port of call. There is nothing wrong with this, except that you have done the work and someone else might get the sale. Keep in mind that customers will buy from someone! There are ways to improve your chances of an enquiring customer returning when they are ready to buy.

This is not done by using silly threats about stock running out, or about rising prices. As I said, no one believes those one-liners anymore. If you have an undecided buyer, your next objective is to make as certain as possible that the customer will return. Salespeople hear the familiar "I'll think about it" or "I'll consult the boss." This means that the buyer is not yet convinced, or they

ADD ON SELLING IS ADVANCED SELLING AND SERVICE

want to shop around, or that there are several others involved in the buying decision. Simply, they are not ready to buy.

Retailers of cars, cameras, computers, appliances and the like, know that most people only buy after two or three visits to about three different stores. We are a nation of shoppers, we love shopping, and we are all keen to get the best buys, the best product and deals. As a professional you can live well with this and use it to your best advantage. Already you have improved the chances of a customer returning by the professional service you have offered. You have 'differentiated' your presentation, company and product. You have done what you can, and done it well, but still find that you cannot close the sale right now.

Following are some useless and inept methods many sellers use when they figure that a sale cannot be made immediately.

'What have I gotta do to get your business right now?' is as dangerous as it is silly. Think about what this suggests. It says that there is a lower price than that which you have just told your customer was the best deal ever. Also, it invites the customer to ask for something you may not be able to do. For example, the customer may nominate a price they know you cannot match. If you ask what you have to do to get the sale, then intrinsically you are confirming the customer's suspicions that they should indeed shop around further; a better deal might be available. This idea is true, whether we're talking about a million dollars' worth of a sale to a company or a $200 camera to a teenager.

Another risky line is to tell a customer who is not ready to buy that you will match whatever price they find. How could you promise this? Once again, you are telling them that the price you quoted as your best deal may not be the best. When you have to let the customer go it is far better to use a positive parting line as I suggested earlier '*Give us a chance when you are ready because* although prices sometimes go up there is an equally good chance that by the time you are ready to buy the price may have gone down.'

Remember to observe your company policies. One of these is to make a profit or else your job might disappear. Some of my suggestions may need a change in company policy, but surely the aim is toward a reasonable profit and customer satisfaction rather than a lost sale.

SWITCHING PRODUCT

This cannot always be done but remember what we said about one of the research questions. The one you need to ask early in the interview is *'What have you seen so far?'* or *'What are you considering at this stage?'* If you use such questions you know whether the customer has shopped around. You also know what product they have seen and get a feel for whether they were impressed with the TX brand. You need to know whether your company is competitive on that item. The reality of selling is that no one in business can offer every single product at the best price. Your business can offer a better deal on some items and perhaps a lesser deal on others. You cannot suddenly, at the end stage of a sale, suggest a new brand or model just because the price the customer has seen on the TX brand is lower than you like or can match.

Sometimes a customer will ask for a product you know your competition is selling at an unprofitable price. This can be due to the competition being overstocked, desperate or simply because they want to meet sales targets. If you twig that a competitor is offering a product at an unprofitable price then this is the time you might try to 'switch' the customer to another product. Switching can be done mainly at an early stage, during the research stage

ADD ON SELLING IS ADVANCED SELLING AND SERVICE

of the sale. This is particularly useful in retail selling. You will have to prove that the alternative you offer is as good or better value. And it better be. This is a subtle technique. You must retain integrity. Only real, confident professionals manage to do this properly.

You must offer good reasons when suggesting another model or brand of product.

This will be difficult if you have not found out what benefits the customer is looking for. If you are using the 'switch technique' it's best to offer a choice of two different items instead of what was initially asked for by the customer. Therefore, you need to know exactly what you are going to say when employing this idea.

Product switch needs to be done early in the sale. Let's say your customer has asked for an LTF model bicycle. You happen to know, because you keep your eye on the market place, that these are being sold by the competition at a very low price. You might proceed by saying something like "The LTF is a very good bicycle, but selling as it does around the $500 mark, I believe it might not represent best value for money. Would you like to see what we think is the best deal currently?" At this point you might recall the 'selling down' idea. Most customers will consider something that will cost them less than the product they initially considered. So this can be a large part of your 'switch' approach.

If the customer shows interest in your offer, go right ahead. If they are not interested in an alternative then all you can do is to offer the best deal you can on the LTF, and build in as many of your companies extra guarantees, services etc. as possible. Switching to another product should never involve you denigrating either another business or another product.

THE CREATIVE SALES GAME

This is a fun and challenging sales game you can do anytime. Sales trainers and managers should use it regularly. It will spice up the day and result in good profits as well as new customers. Each week or month you pick, say, three items from your product range and offer them to just about everyone coming through the door. These items may be accessories, new products or services. You offer just one or two items to each customer. Perhaps you pick two small and one large item. In a bicycle store, for example, there are plenty of great accessories and usually some new model bike that goes faster. When do you offer these? Not before you find out what the customer wants, perhaps as the last word before they leave.

The idea is simple and effective. In a camera store all the salesperson does when facing the customer is to offer something like, 'Have you seen these new leather camera bags?' or 'Did you know that there is a new more powerful zoom lens available for your camera?' That's all there is to it. You make one offer regardless of what they were asking for. Don't harp on it at all. The customers will either show interest or say 'No thanks' in which case you just let it go. I bet many customers will say something like, 'No, I'm not interested in that, but that reminds me that I need a new battery or I might look at such and such.' I've never found customers offended by such suggestions. Some will be interested and for others it will jog their memory about some other product. Either way, your sales figures will go up and so will your profit. You are showing interest in the customer and that is always good.

TEMPLATE OF A SALE; AN EXERCISE

This is a great exercise for a sales team. It should be used monthly. Split the sales team into groups of three. A manager might facilitate the exercise. It can also be done with a small or large group as sales training and should take only 10-20 minutes. It will serve to constructively check and correct sales technique and it is a great motivator and quite good fun.

Each participant rotates in three different roles. The manager only observes and designs the situation. The three roles are:

- A serious customer who should present a certain type of selling situation as designed by the sales manager.

- The salesperson that demonstrates the selling steps using good question and listening techniques.

- Jiminy Cricket, (your conscience and advisor). This role is the silent listener who is advisor to both seller and customer. The manager should not take on this role; it should be one of the sales staff.

The exercise should be kept short and snappy, perhaps 5 minutes. Salespeople can demonstrate only one or two segments of the sale. You are not trying to go through all the selling steps, only the ones that apply to the segment that has been agreed upon. For example, let's say that the person playing the role of the salesperson is asked to demonstrate the step that refers to selling benefits rather than features. In this case you can dispense with all the steps before and after this stage; although you need to go into your research step, there is no need to demonstrate sale closing.

The exercise can be done either using a product actually sold or using a product you don't sell. For example, if you sell fridges you might do the exercise selling life insurance or a bicycle. It may feel a touch artificial initially, but after a few rounds most salespeople find it great fun and a good refresher of their sales training. The customer and seller can call for time-out if they are unsure about how to proceed and consult Jiminy Cricket, the observer, (not the manager).

Do the exercise neither too lightly nor too seriously. Have fun and think. Choose your words and ideas carefully and take time out to consult 'Jiminy Cricket.' At the end of the first round of the game change roles so each of the three people play each role.

Setting up the game

- The person playing the role of customer gives a brief of the situation, the item being sold, and at what point the sale is. The customer should be challenging, but there is no need to be ridiculously objectionable.

- It is the seller's job to use and demonstrate the selling steps to the customer and to 'Jiminy Cricket' – the observer.

ADD ON SELLING IS ADVANCED SELLING AND SERVICE

- Jiminy Cricket says nothing unless asked by either seller or customer in 'time out.' He/she is there to observe and provide *feedback at the end of the exercise* to the seller about what was done well, what was not so good and what was left out. The customer can also offer feedback.

The purpose of this exercise is to let sales staff practice and demonstrate the isolated segments of the agreement summary of selling steps.

- Research stage

Rationale: Make it your business to know more about their business.

- Set objectives for this sale. Your game objective may be about how to close the sale or about how to get an add-on sale or another appointment. Have a secondary objective in mind such as getting the customer to come back later.

Rationale: The more definite the objective or goal for this interview the more likely it is that you get a good result?

- Demonstrate features and benefits. Jiminy should watch this section closely for clues on productive and non-productive discussion.

Rationale: No one buys products but what the product does for them.

- Umbrella technique. Ask questions and summarize all along, every step of the way.

Rationale: How else, but by using questioning and listening would you know what to offer, what to ask for, and how the sale is progressing?

- Handle objections. Use the steps and ways to handle objections rather than just answering them.

Rationale: Many sales are lost for unknown reasons. These are actually reasons you had not found out.

- Listen for buying signals.

Rationale: You can try to close a sale only if you hear buying signals. If not, then test for it before moving on. Otherwise the salesperson will come across as either pushy or as indecisive. Neither is productive.

- Close, propose, or offer to finalize the sale. You must ask for an order or a conclusion.

Rationale: It shows confidence to ask how we are going, and then if in agreement, to ask for the sale.

- Add-on sales. Go for more? Be creative? Or simply shut up, take the order and walk away? No one minds a professional (and sensible) further offer if it adds to the benefits.

Rationale: Most people do not try for that extra sale yet it is good service to do so and it is easy to do.

- Didn't get the sale? Leave the 'door open'. The least you can do is to try and get the customer to come back. This is when we might use one of the **'special' techniques.**

~

I suggest that what most people call selling is just telling and it is an unprofessional and often not so pleasant affair. What I recommend is proper automatic know-how of selling skills and awesome communication techniques. Both are easy to learn, neither is all that mysterious. Before I move on to the next and most important part of my offering I will take a brief look at Selling Bunkums.

CHAPTER 6

THE GREAT, AND SMALL BUNKUMS OF SELLING

A 'bunkum' is an old fashioned word for things that have no validity, no point, and are bad and useless ideas. In the selling profession, bunkums are those very unhelpful behaviours and thinking that work against salespeople. The following are examples of some of the many useless and harmful things salespeople do and say. I suggest that these ways of thinking or talking are sheer bunkum, nonsense, poppycock, and stupidity. Have I communicated my feelings clearly?

Many bunkums come from the inevitability of learning selling by copying sometimes useless and bad techniques from others. Just for the hell of it, see whether some of these bunkums about selling apply equally to your private life. I bet some will.

SELLING IS NOT *JUST* TELLING

Bunkum 1.   You can be anything you want; you can do anything you choose.

This is obviously nonsense, for many reasons. This is a sure fire recipe to make yourself feel like a failure. The crunch is that it is not true that anyone can be or do anything they choose. There are some facts about our personal limitations, be they physical, mental, or related to our situation that restricts our choices. However, the good news is that all of us can improve our lot in life in some ways.

We all have dreams and that's a good thing. But if you don't have what it takes it is no good asking yourself for what you simply cannot do. The better question is – What are my best qualities and how can I maximize these? What else can I learn and use to bring meaning and satisfaction?

Bunkum 2.   Customers are difficult and usually lie.

It may be true that some customers will do a bit of truth bending at times, particularly if they do not feel that you are a professional. Some salespeople act as if the customer is the enemy, rather than the potential friend who pays their salary. This attitude hides an inadequate understanding of selling.

Bunkum 3.   If you tell the customer the entire truth, you won't get the sale.

True enough if your product or deal is not entirely right for the customer. If this is the case then you should not get the sale anyway. How would you feel if you were lied to? Does this mean telling the customer about all the problems of this product and your company? Certainly not. The truth, as information for this customer, is all you need to give. Every product has some draw back, every deal may not be the absolute best possible one, but balance good points against lesser ones, offer compensatory factors and a sale is likely to eventuate.

Customers usually catch out salespeople who do some truth bending and usually won't challenge the sales staff. These customers won't buy; they just politely say 'thanks for the information' and walk away. Since the salesperson doesn't know what has happened, he/she is left with no idea why the sale did not materialize. Customers are more perceptive than many salespeople realize.

Bunkum 4. *Customers are out to save every last cent.*

You might think that nearly all customers want to get just one thing, a better price. Well, you do when you are a customer! But this is not entirely true. *Customers mainly want to make a satisfactory purchase from a company and salesperson they can trust.* Get your presentation right and watch customers come back; sometimes they may even pay a little more to deal with you – if they like you. And they will like you if you are a professional, and that, by the way, is all they have to like you for, (you don't need to be cute).

Very ordinary salespeople spend their time whining about their pricing difficulties. Good sellers know that *the moment the discussion is about price then they are very close to making a sale.* Certainly, everyone wants a good deal, but a 'good deal' is not only about the lowest price.

Bunkum 5. *The look of the customer determines their price range.*

This simply is not true. Neither age, nor gender, nor dress or any other factors will tell you anything about their price range. Only your good research questions will indicate the price range that is right for this customer, not the way they look.

Bunkum 6.   Customers often say, 'I'll have to think about it.'

True enough but if they have to 'think about it' that means you simply have not convinced them to buy. It is possible that they are not yet ready to buy for their own reasons.

Bunkum 7.   All salespeople need to do is be friendly.

Yes that may help if customers think you're genuine. The customer wants expertise and a good interview buying experience. Being attentive is friendly enough. Being too familiar, cute, silly etc. can be offensive. The customer has a focus, stay with that. How friendly you need to be depends on the customer's personality type and communication style. (Soon we'll come to that major issue).

Bunkum 8.   It is good to copy other more experienced salespeople.

If you are very lucky you might get to work with a real professional. Even then just copying is tricky because you are you, not them. It is a good thing to observe successful sellers and take on some of their techniques, *but you need to adapt them to your personality and situation.* It takes thought and action to see what your personality can use properly. The danger is that by watching and copying others you can easily slip into the other person's bad selling habits. Even *good technique needs adaptation.* A young salesperson won't be able to communicate some things in the same way as an older one might, or the other way around. Imagine my 60-yearold face using 'cool' language to a 20-year-old.

Bunkum 9.   You must always tell the entire truth to everyone.

This too can be a disaster. The fact is that we need to answer others honestly, but to tell customers that what they can afford is only half as good as the best, is not necessary. There is no need to say that in a few more months the price of TV sets might be less. Leave out your personal opinion when discussing colour, size or shape. What do you do, if you know a particular product is junk? Don't sell it!

Bunkum 10. *Never give the customer your best deal first up.*

This is playing with fire. Many customers will shop around and if they get a better deal elsewhere they may never come back and you will never know why.

Offering the best deal first up sometimes seems to be a problem for salespeople, but look at it this way, if you offer your best deal first and the customer goes away there is good reason to think that the competition will offer it at around the same deal/price. If you did a professional job of the sales presentation, many people will come back even if only to tell you that your deal was beaten. You will get a second chance, particularly if you build into your presentation one of the techniques outlined under the heading of 'Special Sales Techniques.'

Bunkum 11. *Making assumptions about customers.*

Any and all assumptions you make about a customer may be totally incorrect unless you have done the research steps well.

Some of these assumptions are that customers do, or do not know, what they want, are not ready to buy, have been shopping around and will shop around further. Or that they only want to pay a certain amount, or that they have a lot of technical information or too little and so on. *Don't assume anything. Always check it out before you take action.*

Bunkum 12. People buy things only from people they like.

The great bunkum of this is the opposite, namely when you claim that the customer did not like you, you had a 'personality clash.' Being liked by the new customer is neither a mystery nor just luck. If you want to be liked then give the customer something they can like – a professional presentation.

Bunkum 13. Closing the sale is hard.

Nonsense, and horse manure. This is actually the easiest thing to do if...you did all you needed to do before. But you must finalize the sale. You can only be afraid of being knocked back when closing a sale if you do not feel that you have earned the sale. *It is a simple matter of asking, making an offer or helping to make a decision.* You are not asking customers for a life changing decision.

All you are doing when closing a sale is helping the customer make a buying decision.

So take it easy and do it easy. Keep it simple *and know how you are going to ask for the sale.* 'No one can win them all' is true, but only if you have actually tried to close the sale.

Bunkum 14. I can make up for lost sales, lost time and lost opportunities.

I'm afraid not. Whatever you did not do yesterday, sold or enjoyed or did not enjoy, is gone, it is lost. Do not dwell on it, that is useless, but do learn from it. *Do not fool yourself; there is no making up for anything.* Not even for not having started improving your sales technique – then again don't worry about why you have not started yet, just do it now.

Bunkum 15. I'll never see this customer again so nothing matters but making the sale.

The fact is that your best customers are the ones who return and recommend you to someone else. *You want to make customers not just sales.* This is vital. You will never know how many of your successful sales have come from happy customers, but many will. In any case, being a professional and of service to others will give you a better feeling about yourself and your job.

Bunkum 16. There is no need to use all the selling steps every time.

You are kidding only your sweet self. Perhaps there are times when a step can be left out, maybe when talking with a repeat customer with whom you have an established relationship. You know them and if they know lots about your product, then you might leave out a step or two. Generally, however, you must always use every step. If you leave a step out you must still check that what was left out was covered using summary listening in case you have misread the situation.

For example, in industrial selling cycles some customers know more technical details about a product than the salesperson does. In this case you could leave out talking about benefits that come from such features. Perhaps! You must still check that your customers do, in fact, understand, and that must be done with care to make sure your client does not think you are telling the bleeding obvious.

Bunkum 17. It is always obvious what benefits the customer wants.

That would be nice, but it is untrue. Many *customers are not sure what benefits they want or need, or which benefits are the most important to their situation.* Some customers will look and sound like they are definite about the benefits they want, but be wary. It is up to you to unearth the benefits that best fit this customer. No one ever buys products for just one benefit. There are always several issues, some matter more and some less.

A simple example from the photo trade is when we ask what the customer is looking for. Most will tell us they just want nice photos. Many salespeople are fooled by this and move on to other issues or to presenting a camera too soon. You need more information, such as what specific things they want to photograph. Are there children involved in sports? Will they use it for business? Do they like taking people pictures or scenery?

Bunkum 18. *Customers who have many objections are a pain and probably won't buy.*

Wrong. These are the very people who are in fact interested in your product. Someone who raises several objections may be more interested than someone who has no objections. It is usually the very people who raise no objections who say 'thank you for your help' and walk out leaving you wondering where you went wrong.

Bunkum 19. *You must always try to sell a more expensive product.*

How do you feel when someone does that to you? Probably suspicious of the salesperson unless there are good reasons that make instant sense to you. It is best to fit the price range to the customer's needs and ability to pay. *Research what they want and need and then sell them the best fit they can afford.* Being genuine is always remembered. So is being greedy.

THE GREAT, AND SMALL BUNKUMS OF SELLING

Bunkum 20. It is okay to talk to other salespeople while you are talking with the customer.

Oh man, oh man – or woman for that matter. This should be hardly worth a mention and yet you see it so often. It is an absolute no-no to let a customer wait while you talk to another staff member, other than beyond a couple of words, and then only if you are helping the other salesperson with their job. A couple of words, not four sentences. Never ignore customers. If you must keep them waiting then instantly acknowledge that you won't be long.

Bunkum 21. You can't serve more than one customer at a time in retail.

Yes you can. In a busy retail environment most people will wait for a while if they are being served. You can excuse yourself and answer the phone briefly. Customers hate the sound of an un-answered phone while they are talking to you. You can also acknowledge a waiting customer, but get back to your active customer really quickly. Customers will happily wait while they have a product in their hands. In fact, they like being left alone with the item for a short while.

Bunkum 22. Many products only have features and you cannot readily demonstrate the benefit.

There is nothing for sale in this world that does not have demonstrable benefits. Some products may require a creative approach when it comes to demonstrating the benefits. You must have tangible benefits to show whether you are selling a cleaning service, a trip to the moon, or a cure for the common cold. Demonstrate what you can, show samples, show proven outcomes, explain everything in terms of benefits.

SELLING IS NOT *JUST* TELLING

Bunkum 23. 'Oh gosh you look good in that.'

Most people won't believe you. Shallow one-liners alienate many customers. Say positive things only if you mean them, keep silent if you do not. It is only a matter of opinion anyway. Sincerity smells right while manure... well you know what that smells like.

Bunkum 24. You cannot be yourself when selling.

You cannot be anyone else but you. The thing is *you must use that part of you that is a selling professional*. The other bits of you, the mum, the cook, the long suffering employee, your bad knees etc. can take a rest for now. Genuine people are liked even if they do not have all the information or total technical expertise. Sometimes new salespeople do really well at the start by being just who they are. It is easy to slip into the 'selling role' but it is far better to be real; just your little old self.

Bunkum 25. It does not matter who the customer is, you always treat them in the same way.

How could this be true? Everyone is an individual and you must treat them as such. If you try to sell to everyone in exactly the same way you will get bored and lose sales. You do not deal or communicate with your friends or relatives in exactly the same way. Everyone's personality will be different and what they perceive as benefits when purchasing may differ. You cannot sell a camera to a teenager in the same way as you would to a pro photographer or to the buyer setting up a TV station. Treat everyone as unique. *The selling techniques are always the same but each customer is different.*

Bunkum 26.   You cannot change your body language.

You can, but only if you become aware of what your body language is saying. This is not done by play acting or pretending. Working out what and how to go about changing will be possible once you are aware of what you need to change.

Bunkum 27.   Ignore other customers if you are busy.

If a friend calls on you, do you keep them waiting without a word or a nod until you have finished your dinner? Hopefully not without at least saying 'I won't be long.' It is just the same when a customer comes into a store and you are busy. Acknowledge them immediately, at least. There is nothing worse than customers waiting for salespeople who are filing bits of paper, or for any reason. A busy place suggests a good business. And never say "I won't be long mate, buddy, love" etc.

Bunkum 28.   'I'm only in this job until I get discovered as a great ...'

I hope the big break happens for you, but in the meantime *you may as well be good at what you are doing right now.* Being a pro at anything will make you better at everything. It is a bit like going to the gym. It is 'training,' even if you finish up doing something different. Be good at selling, it is what you do no matter what you are doing anyway! If your boss does not see how good you are someone else will.

Bunkum 29.   Some customers are angry and looking for a fight, so it wasn't your fault that there was a 'personality clash.'

Oh yes it is, it is you who got hooked! If an agitated customer confronts you, you must try and side step, rather than get hooked into the customer's frame of mind. They may be negative, you can't afford to be. Use your professional attitude; it is likely that a sale will eventuate if you keep your cool.

Bunkum 30.   *You've got no time to work out how to manage your time.*

Have I got your attention here? There is something drastically wrong about the way people spend their time. You must manage your time at work and at play. Less stress will occur and more will get done.

Bunkum 31.   *It is a good question to ask an undecided customer: 'What do I have to do to get this sale?'*

This is a counter-productive and boring question. The idea behind the question may appear okay, but look at what you are actually asking and/or suggesting. Some customers, like me, will tell you what you have to do and it is usually something unrealistic.

Instead of that bad question you may need to take a step back using the summary listening techniques to confirm the things the customer liked about the product and the deal so far. This reinforces agreement and gives the customer another chance to agree to buy.

Bunkum 32.   *You believe that the services and guarantees your company offers are not enough or not the right ones.*

Don't concentrate on what you don't have to offer. Instead, use what you do have in the best possible way. All businesses offer various guarantees and services. The marketing done by your company is often wasted and is rarely used properly by salespeople. Smart salespeople use every single advantage their company markets and advertises. If you really believe that your company's deals are not good enough then consider finding other employment.

Bunkum 33. People on the phone often waste your time.

No, the contrary in fact. Callers are interested to find out what you can offer them in respect to what they need or want. Putting your best foot forward on the phone will result in customers coming to see you, very likely as immediate buyers, because you have already established a good relationship. The customer on the phone will hear and pick up your attitude. Customers hearing you helpful on the phone will have confidence in what you say. Welcome callers; ask them to see you in person.

Big Bunkum 34. The 'As if...'syndrome.

Though I have already covered this, it is worth re telling. 'As if,' is a deeper going bunkum, a more personally psychological issue that many people do not recognize. We all know someone we call a 'bloody know all.' Unfortunately, many people can be like that.

People do and say things 'as if' they knew. 'As if', is partially magical thinking and partially play-acting. Most people are very tolerant of salespeople who own up to 'No, I do not know' or 'I do not understand.' Always offer to find out what they need to know.

If you are uncertain about what the customer wants or needs you must ask for clarification or the sale cannot, and must not proceed. *Sales are lost due to 'as if' understanding of the customers real needs.*

Bunkum 35. *If the customer asks for something you do not have, or do not offer, it is okay to politely say that you are sorry, and let them go.*

Never say no and leave it at that. You are making a gross mistake unless of course you sell cameras and they are asking for shoes. If you do not have what they ask for, suggest alternatives but don't be long winded or pushy. You could ask what results and benefits they were actually looking for. The least you can do is to show interest. Do not push if the customer says no, but do this well and the customer might come back another time. Some customers will listen others won't. If you don't show any interest you can be certain they will never come back.

Bunkum 36. *to 1,000,000*

Find some more bunkums yourself, it won't be hard. You know in your bones many of these inept things are pointless.

CHAPTER 7

ENHANCED PROFESSIONAL SELLING, MARKETING AND PROMOTING & HIGH QUALITY PERSONAL AND BUSINESS COMMUNICATIONS

PERSONALITY TYPES AND STYLES

The selling techniques and the communication and relationship practices we have discussed so far, work a lot better if you have the right understanding of what makes you and other people tick. That seems obvious, but what is less obvious is how do you quickly assess other people with

> This chapter may be the most important section in this book.

reasonable accuracy in the selling situation? Even trickier, how well do you know yourself when and where it matters? I mean, we all know ourselves to a point, but what are the triggers that we have and can use – or should be wary of – and how do we get more familiar with these?

One of the things that keep us from understanding more about ourselves is that we do not have a user-friendly way to conceptualize ideas about human behaviour. The better we can conceptualize that, the more we can make it work for us every day in every way. I have borrowed this idea from the great thinker, Einstein. I paraphrase one of his famous sayings: 'Scientific exploration cannot proceed further until what is being investigated is conceptualized.' Until you can hypothesize some sort of theory of personality – your own and your customer's – until then, you cannot improve the way you communicate and achieve what you want.

After more than forty years of selling products and ideas, I can only confirm what everyone knows about doing business or running any organization – your business is as good as the people who work in it. This chapter explores ways of getting to know yourself and others better. Some clarity about the way people operate and communicate can be signposted, up to a point. The ability to understand yourself and others quickly and correctly in a given situation is not just a great advantage but also a better way to enjoy the selling business, and relationships with both employees and customers.

> Those who think making a sale, getting an agreement or finding a solution is a matter of luck or liking are certainly not maximizing their chances. *Understanding personality types and styles are what true professionals use to their best advantage, activating excellent powers of communication.*

Automatic competence of the selling steps and the questioning and listening techniques make certain that you are being helpful, offering professional service and that you get not just a sale but an ongoing relationship with the customer. *However, the techniques work best if you are an outstanding communicator because there are many different personality types.* Nevertheless (or more), we can signal what a particular person might be like when purchasing something if we have at least a basic understanding of personality types and communication styles.

The starting point to awesome communication and sales skills is to become familiar with how you operate and what your personality type and communication style is.

Until that's done you can't move on to understanding your customer's styles and types. Only a reasonable basis of understanding is needed, you don't have to become a psychologist. A good grasp of the idea will make a big difference and ensure that you communicate with people as individuals rather than treating them just as 'customers.'

What we see, hear or miss, is vital not only at the moment of first impression but right through the sale. You receive information through sight, words and body language. All these can be badly misread and are misunderstood by salespeople. Conversely, the customer can misunderstand you, if you are not careful. In life, we make decisions about another person within seconds of meeting them. In retail stores, you have about 1 sec to 15 minutes to forge a buying relationship. Recall the saying: "You only get one chance to make a first impression."

During the first few minutes in a selling situation, you and your prospective customer form opinions about each other, often without being aware you have done so. Your impressions create an instant feeling about other people. I repeat that much of *this first impression is not in your awareness; it is sort of a feeling you may not immediately notice.* No one is totally closed to changing these opinions later, but if you get or give the wrong impression initially, then you will have twice the work to do.

Salespeople often lose the customer with or without knowing why. Sometimes they say it was a 'personality clash.' This is due to a lack of understanding of personality types and communication styles.

PERSONALITY 'TYPES' HAVE CERTAIN 'COMMUNICATION STYLES' ATTACHED TO THEM.

There are two important, separate, but interrelated issues here. Each depends on the other. We all have a personality. Rich or poor, successful or not, everyone has a way, a particular style of communication that is seen by others. 'Personality' is sometimes also referred to as the 'ego' – a wide and complex term. I will stick with the word 'personality' because that expresses what I am concerned with. Personality incorporates all the qualities that make you act, think and feel the way you do. Even though *the appearance of communication styles differ from one person to another, it still shows* some common and recognizable traits. It is these common traits you can understand and address in order to best communicate with others.

Parts of the communication style presented to the world are easy to see. Stay with me while I state the obvious. For example, a person with a shy personality type does not act in gregarious, loud ways; it's just not their style. A person with an outgoing personality type likes lots of people contact; their style will show more interest in others. A quiet person may be a better listener, while an impatient person may not be interested in friendly or lengthy discussions. I could go on with the list but wait, there really is more to contemplate. There are several broadly based different personality types. I want to offer a simplified way of quickly distinguishing the various types and the styles that are attached to them.

> Any explanation about personality types is aimed at understanding the particular communicating styles that are attached to them.

I am restricted in how far I can go into this in a short book about selling, so I have concentrated this exploration on the more obvious sorts of personality types and styles; the ones that are most important to recognize in the selling business... and in private life. There is enough common ground between people to help us get to know ourselves and others better and more quickly by being familiar with at least the basic personality types and styles. Of course, I hasten to add, people cannot really be sorted into a few only types of personalities, the variations can be mind-boggling.

PERSONALITY 'SOLUTIONS'

There is that word again 'SOLUTIONS.' I have used that word and the word BENEFIT and OUTCOME more than 200 times in this work. For that, finding right solutions to our needs and wants is the one and only issue in life.

Is change possible? Do people really change? I don't need to go into this heavily as there are lots of arguments on the subject. *It seems to me that we are more likely to change our 'styles' than our personality types.* This is what experts call a behavioural, cognitive approach. A change in style however, is likely to bring a change in the basic personality type as well. Not always, but possibly.

In order to arrive at certain perceived benefits for themselves people tend to have certain 'solutions' they believe will be helpful to get what they want.

Some of these so called solutions turn out to be no solutions at all, (or worse), but they were supposed to have been the answer. Many were developed without awareness in early childhood, some were 'chosen' later, but such choices may have been made knowingly or without any consciousness. Several, perhaps even most, were inherited from parents, culture and the society around us. Some values and ideas that drive us were established as we grew up and may not be easily changed, but *our behaviour-solutions are more open to change.*[1]

Note, yet again, that the word 'solutions' always refers to people looking for a 'benefit' – the very concept and essence of selling. Just look how this holds true regarding early childhood. Children look for solutions by behaving in certain ways, or to put it bluntly the kids just want what they want; what they see as benefits.

---

[1] I will be publishing a more extended exploration on personality types, styles and personal relationships in 2014-2015.

Unfortunately, not all seeming solutions turn out to be real benefits, not even in adult life!

Recall that features are what bring benefits or solutions.

The communication styles you employ are driven by your personality as we have said. *How you came to be the way you are was also driven by your inherent features.* Every human being has certain features some of which cannot be changed. You know a lot of your features, but you may have others you are not aware of. What you have done with your features, what you are using is variable and dependent on many factors around you such as parental influence, the society into which you were born, opportunity etc.

Just about any feature that you developed as a potential solution to the world around you as a child, and later as an adult, can be a good thing in the right dosage depending on what we are talking about. *For example, a certain propensity to push and press others can be a good 'feature' bringing the benefit of getting things done. An overdose of the same quality might lead to stepping on people, inconsiderate behaviour and lots of aggravation.*

One of the things I will suggest later is that you can change your communication style to a more successful one by finding and using those features of your personality, which work best for your situation.

What made you how you are; the development of the personality.

Personality develops as a result of past experiences, genetic givens, social and parental input, and on the current environment and situation. The process starts from day one (or even earlier) and goes on for a lifetime. There is agreement that much of the personality is set in stone long before the 21st year. Many psychologists tend to agree that most of our personality is programmed before the age of three.

Your basic personality type and style is probably similar at various stages of life. For example, your type and style was similar enough in many ways between the ages of say 20 and 30, and perhaps between 40 and 50 years of age. But it is not static; it may keep changing, often surprisingly, while you are not looking – if you know what I mean.

The famous post Freudian psychologist, Karen Horney, explained what I am getting at in regard to how people become who they are, and how they unknowingly choose certain behaviour or solutions in their lives. Much of what I offer as a practical and user-friendly model of personality types comes from her framework. Some of it is from a Melbourne psychologist, Don Treacher, leader of the Cairnmillar Institute's program called 'Human Relationships for Everyday Living.' To these foundations I have added much learning from other experts in the fields of psychology and philosophy and also my personal experience as it refers to the selling profession.

Children react to parental, social and environmental situations and unknowingly choose one of the following three 'movements' as Horney called them. These movements simply mean that the child has a certain propensity toward a particular type of solution. Horney called these *three movements or solutions 'moving toward' 'moving against' and 'moving away.'* The movements are neither good nor bad as such, in themselves. The point is not so much that any one of the movements is better. All of them have good and bad aspects. In general, everyone has a dose of all three movements.

Problems can arise when we are firmly stuck in any one solution/movement. Being stuck in any one of the three positions is called over identifying, or alternately, disowning. Neither over identification or disowning parts of yourself brings good life solutions. Both restrict full expression of talents, needs and wants and the ability to think and feel clearly. The result is fewer real choices and a more restricted way of life. *It is important to* note that each movement has toxic elements as well as corresponding healthy ones.

Our solutions were determined by the values imbedded in us in our young years. We unknowingly, in the main, settled on solutions that are driven by dominant values. For example, if parents put a great value on being nice and never showing anger, then their children are likely to opt for the 'moving towards' solution. This always being 'nice' can be over identifying with the idea of reasonable cooperation with others. If there was value placed on aggression, efficiency and hard work, the children are likely to select the 'moving against' solutions.

This is disowning of the loving, cooperative-nice self and over identifying with being assertive, usually winding up being over aggressive. If the child experienced that neither of these solutions worked well, then they may have opted for the 'moving away' solution. Neither being 'nice' or 'assertive aggressive' worked, so it appears as if the only solution is not to get too involved with others. So we accepted a certain value system, which we added to, and hopefully changed as we grew up, sometimes only by making a serious effort to do so. *We can only effect change if and once we are* aware of our actions, motivations and style.

I shall further outline the three 'movements' and how they might operate. Then we can extend the idea to personality types and to the communication styles which attach to them, and how these show up in selling. I will apply these ideas to practical selling and to everyday personal communications. By necessity and in order to keep this exploration straightforward, I have not gone into every reason why a child may have 'chosen' a certain position. When I say 'chosen' it is not quite the right word for choice implies freedom and knowledge that children do not usually have. Many factors may prevail such as split families, wars, a hard life, not so good parenting or an over cautious one, too much or too little loving, and much more. Let's now consider in some more detail the three main positions. While you are reading this see if you can relate to any or several of the positions but don't be too hasty in labelling yourself.

'Moving Toward' is the 'Deferrer' solution

On the negative side this is the harmony seeking, deferring to others at all costs solution. This is where a child (unknowingly) decided that they will only get what they need from parents and others by being sweet and lovable all the time no matter how they feel. Thus feeling assertive or demanding is left out of interactions with people. As adults, these people as buyers may not tell you how they really feel, won't challenge, or voice dissatisfaction, and are likely to keep silent and leave without buying if they are not well looked after. *These customers, like all others, need to feel that they can trust the salesperson, but these people need that trust even more than the other types of customers.*

Parents who are too demanding, dogmatic or perhaps just convinced that children have to be over controlled are likely to bring on this situation. When this sort of 'movement' is bedded in, and children grow up with this as the underlying 'solution' to life situations, they can be said to be *over identified* with it. The result is that the growing child, and later the adult, lose healthy powers of assertive behaviour. In personal life they feel they cannot live without getting and giving 'love' no matter how they actually feel about what is being done to and around them. Earlier I said that most of us do not 'choose' in the real sense of the word any of the movements, but the true deferrer uses this one style as a way of expressing his/her life situation, their needs and wants. Such a solution restricts certain qualities leading possibly to a restricted selection of what one might personally achieve.

There is a healthy side of the 'moving toward – deferrer' solution and that is the ability to love and care for others, to be able to feel affection.

If a person has a reasonable identification to this type of movement rather than an over-investment, they can offer and gain love, peace and harmony in reasonable proportions. Get this right and you can be great at peace making, negotiating, personal relating and so on.

'Moving Against' is the 'Demander' solution

The 'demander' style is a more aggressive, arrogant solution. Where there is insufficient control of boundaries set by parents the young child manages to get on top of the parents and others by screaming and yelling or whatever. The child learns that being pushy and aggressive works. Aggressive parents also may finish up with aggressive children. Insufficient parenting, lack of or too strict boundaries can also result in a demanding style.

In the adult, this type of solution manifests in selfish and aggressive mannerism and communication style resulting in not enough care for others. The moving against-demander type thinks mainly of themselves and expects others to fall in with their wants and needs. The true demander needs the unquestioned admiration and approval of others.

The negative side brings a demanding, the 'world owes me' type of attitude. The healthy positive side is having a feeling of some proper, if limited, personal power. This brings an ability to use assertive (not aggressive) styles of communications and behaviours, resulting in an enhanced ability to get things done.

As customers, if well balanced, these people make decisions based on professional advice and are easy to deal with. If they are over identified with being a demander, these customers willneed careful handling, as they are likely to become aggressive, angry and demanding if they don't get what they expect. Sometimes they expect what they truly cannot have. On the positive side, this style of conduct helps them to ask for what they need, or to say what they do not like or want. They can be great leaders, action and change makers.

'Moving Away' is the 'Defector' solution

Although I said before that none of the positions are better or worse, in some ways this one can be a trickier position than the previous two, for both as customers and as relationship partners these people are likely to bail out on you if and when problems arise. That is their solution; to defect, to leave the situation. The defector's solution is a 'who cares anyway, I'm okay on my own' personality and way of life. If neither of the 'toward-deferrer' or the 'against-demander' solution worked well, then children will shut up, withdraw and live too much within themselves. They emotionally move away or 'defect' from relating to others.

If you had two angry parents who fought a lot with each other, you may have chosen the away defector solution as your way of answering the incoming threat and confusion of parental anger. Or perhaps there was just too much disappointment or fear in the early years. As adults, defector types are loners, shy, and tend to not be too involved in anything that involves others; they'd rather not get involved at all: they defect. Still, they need other people, not just for everyday living, but also so that they can repeat *the sad scenario, which is to be able to move toward or against someone and then defect from them.* These people are likely to find it hard to have commitment to intimate or deeper relationships with others. The positive end of the away-defector movement is a healthy ability to be okay on their own. The negative end is potentially an isolated and lonely life. As customers these people can be hard to read and they tend to be highly suspicious of salespeople. Be too friendly and they will hate it. If they think you don't care, they leave very fast, but if you make it safe for them you have them as solid customers.

Transactional Analysis

It will help to better understand the above ideas by looking at another interesting model of personality types and styles. This model comes from Eric Berne's book called "I'm O.k. You're O.k." and it is called Transactional Analysis (TA). I see TA as rather similar to Karen Horney's three pronged movement theory in many ways.

Berne suggested that people (unknowingly) choose one of four life style positions. Three of the four possible positions offered in TA correspond to and help explain the 'movements' in Horney's scheme. Berne's positions show basic underlying assumptions about the self from which we act and deal with life. *Each position is an underlying assumption and presses us to use only certain types of solutions.*

The positions or assumptions nominated by Berne but with my additions are:

'I'm not ok you're ok'

This is similar to the 'toward-deferrer' movement. If you adopted this basic assumption you tend to think that everyone else is better, that others know things and have better life solutions than you do. You believe that only loving and giving-in no matter what, is the way to get what you need. Anger and healthy assertion are out. After all, others have got it right you haven't.

'I'm ok you're not ok'

This corresponds to the 'against-demander' movement and is just the reverse of the previous. This is the assumption of being superior, and therefore, having the right to demand from others and from the world, acting as if others are not as good as you.

Others should see and admire you, but watch out – if you don't get them they'll get you. This position is a self-righteous attitude where showing aggression and anger is power and the only way to control life; yours and theirs.

'I'm not ok and you're not ok'

This is similar to the 'away-defector' movement. It is reflected in the attitude that you don't have things right, but neither do others. No one, yourself included, can be trusted or relied on. Better to stay on your own, give little, and get little. Commit to nothing, you are fine by yourself. The result, if taken to its end degree, is a life likely lacking fulfilment and achievement.

'I'm ok you're ok'

This is Berne's fourth position that Horney does not directly suggest as such. Horney's view appears to be that if one had a healthy mix of three movements: Toward, Against, Away, then the balance would bring in the positive side of each movement to the fore. That is to say, if you are not over-invested in any one movement, then the whole personality is able to act in a spontaneous and fruitful manner using parts of itself that best work in a given situation.

'I'm ok, you are ok' maybe a bit idealistic but it is clearly a good thing to aim for.

It shows a trust of self and others. There is ability to use healthy assertion in positive rather than in aggressive ways, and there is ability to offer and accept affection.

In general, people are looking for pleasure, happiness, good results, meaning, satisfaction; benefits by any other name. What actually brings these results is variable. How people get the satisfactions they look for emanates from, is born out of the life solutions they had settled for.

Unfortunately, people tend to bed-in their 'solutions' even more as they get older, they get more dogmatic.

We can work toward building better life solutions only if we know how we operate in the world.

We are mainly concerned here with doing better business. I have kept the above explanations as brief and as jargon free as possible. For those of you who are interested in looking further and deeper, I have listed the sources of the information and some suggested reading at the end of the book.

No one is just one type or style.

No one is just one of these types or styles in any and every situation. Still, when it comes to making a buying decision or doing something more than say, just going for a walk, it is likely that one or two of the above types and the corresponding styles that go with them will kick in.

So then, how does a deferrer, the harmony seeking type, use his or her own particular solution and ways to be successful in business? As sellers usually these people make a good enough living, but often find it hard to be really good at the business of selling given that their main concern is to be everyone's friend. Deferrers hate confrontation and have trouble in properly asserting themselves at the right times. Closing the sale therefore, does not come easily. A truly deferring type does not like risk taking all that much unless the risk involved can be a harmony filled one, and what kind of risk is that? No risk at all, chances are. As customers deferrers are cautious and will not say all that they feel, if anything at all. They won't discuss what they see as problems or trouble or challenge salespeople.

The demander is an excitement seeking assertive style and will cut through anything in his or her way if it is possible to do so. They probably have more staying power, are likely to be good at looking at opportunities, but their people powers will be at the lower end, unless people around them fit their profile and are not too competitive. Competition concerns the demander, but does not stop them. In personal life, they will seek to have the best relationship ever, but as usual, to their own style and recipe. To get results in life, sometimes one might need to have the sort of single mindedness and push the demander employs. Sometimes they go too far though, believing that the means may be used to justify the ends. This is a potentially precarious way to be handling other people or building relationships.

As salespeople, the demander-excitement seeker may be good at long range planning, at the bigger picture and at selling, but they are less likely to pay sufficient attention to all the necessary details. They will enthuse others, may even be good leaders, although at times lesser people managers. They have less awareness of other people and may not see what others need or want – or even care about that. In their loving relationships or when they are customers they appear to be exciting people at first, but they see little need to bother with working on their relationships unless offered much constant admiration to prop up their actually over sensitive egos. Still, they do make buying decisions faster and will stick with the seller if they find him/ her a professional.

The away-defector types will want to have a kind of checklist about a potential relationship, be that a personal or a business one. In business or in private life, they are likely to be picky and not easy to satisfy. Does this mean they won't be as good at selling or at business? Most likely they are not in the selling business. Defectors can miss the bigger picture, do not like risk taking, are not highly creative, and unlikely to be good motivators. On the other hand, many defectors are good at the small picture where extra efficiency and detail are needed. Some technical areas of selling suit this personality profile.

Everyone has bad and good sides to their personality. Every human trait – just about – can be useful if properly channelled and may be used to good or bad ends. It is the degree and adaptation of our personality traits and styles that matter. Each personality type may be better adapted to selling, if one creatively uses those parts of the personality that best fit the job. Let's look at how understanding of the personality types and communication styles that they produce affect the business of selling.

Are you supposed to change your personality type for every different customer?

You may be wondering by now if you are supposed to change your ways or be an expert reader of other's personality in a magical way. Not to worry. It all may seem daunting to start with but it is all simple enough once it is understood and once you actually KNOW how and what to look for. Of course there is no way you can or should change your personality type and communication style for each new customer.

> Adapt a style that will suit each particular customer – you can do this, once you have some understanding of what style they prefer and like.

This will come easily enough if you are aware of how you present to another person. Hello, Hello, we all think we know how we present to others and how they see us but I can assure you that most of us do not know it so well, and we are greatly and often mistaken when we think that others sees us in a certain way. Now, this may not be our problem as such, but it can be if our view of ourselves is rather different to our client's because this is where we may well 'clash.' So if we can present in a way that suits this particular client better then why not?

We have an image of the stereotypical salespeople. It is no accident and unfortunately, it ain't a good image folks! I wonder if this common view is because the salespeople's personality is similar? I can immediately assure you that this is not correct. But, do people pick the same professions because they have similar personalities? It is more likely, and obvious if you observe it, that many salespeople have copied silly selling habits and modes of communicating from each other! It is a human trait, and often a useful one, to do such copying, but sometimes it is a disaster. It is interesting to note that we never think we copy others, let alone know that we have copied unsuccessful actions. This again is as true at home as it is in business. It's as if all camera salespeople, real estate agents, car salespeople etc are cut from the same cloth, cloned as it were. But this is not so. They have simply copied the behaviours and bad habits of those they saw around them in their particular business, doing their jobs. Knowing what you are doing: the selling steps and this briefing of personality types and styles, will help you to stay away from doing that bad copy, and will keep you far more new and interested in your job as well.

> Various types of customers/people are enthused by various things when buying a product or an idea.

Think about what motivates you when purchasing something. What sorts of words or actions do you like or hate? What sort of body language do you find a put off or inviting? Let's look at this quickly and simply for a start because it is an exciting part of our explorations.

What follows is *a brief summary of the basic styles of communications customers tend to use.* We might say that these customers might be groupings of people who are looking for 'solutions' from their own orientations. They are looking, or operating from, particular feelings and thought patterns expressed as their individual communication styles.

Moving Toward Deferrer customers

The 'toward-deferrer' is a friendly type and style of customer. These people prefer to be served in a personable and friendly manner. They want to believe that the seller is their 'friend' and can be trusted. Not that they would ever admit, or know it, but these customers are looking for products that will make them appear more attractive or desirable. Perhaps they like buying things that they can proudly lend to others or use to enhance their relationships. In any case, they do not like buying goods and may not always be certain as to their own motivation for doing so.

A friendly personable approach is required along with solid assurance of after sales service. These clients do not want trouble, nobody does, but these people really want to be in peace and for this reason the like quality and reassurance. Since they are more compliant, these people are less likely to argue, complain or challenge the deal offered. They are also often the people who thank you for your help and leave without buying. Deferrers won't tell you how they really feel about what you are trying to sell them, unless you are really suitable and with it for their styles. If you do not get the sale you may never know what went wrong. Pushy or flashy selling will really put them off. You need to be more sensitive, more patient and careful with these customers. Any concerns about the product, your company or the way you handle the toward-deferrer, and they are gone, usually thanking you lots for your help, but not purchasing.

If they do buy, these people become your loyal customers sending their friends to you. These buyers dislike being challenged or caught out; most people do. They won't argue or confront you to any extent and get offended fairly easily when challenged, or if they feel put down. For example, if they don't understand what you have said and they ask for more explanation, how you respond may rub them the wrong way if you don't choose the right words and tone.

Deferrers, like any of the other types, can be old or young, conservative or 'New Age.' They just want to be liked and are all heart and kindness. They want, need, and crave commitment therefore they are very interested in guarantees and service. Risk is not liked, but they may take some, if in the end 'harmony or loving' seems an outcome. These customers will likely do their buying research thoroughly so take care that you do your sales presentation properly and in accord with the facts and the customers' communication style. *One important way of doing that, and this is true about dealing with any type of client, is that as a seller you constantly check to see if the customer is with you and be ready to back up into an earlier phase of your selling steps if necessary.* Proof of what you offer is a necessity with all customers, but even more with the deferrer.

When you ask for the sale you need to be gentle. A jokey approach may be fine, rather than sounding even a little pushy. *Couch your sale closing in terms that includes them.* For example, *"Have we found what you are looking for?"* or *"How does this one seem to you?"* Sometimes you need to help them make a decision and if possible you should do this by reiterating that there is little risk in buying this product from you because....

Moving against-demander customers

This customer seeks and likes enthusiastic communication styles and exciting solutions. These people may strongly ask for (demand) what they expect. They love new products and the leading edge of technology. They are likely to hold firmer opinions that you must not directly challenge. They expect top service and deference from the salespeople. Do not start by calling them (or anyone else) 'mate' as this could be deadly. The 'against-demander' type of buyer rarely wants all or too many details unless they are in some highly technical industry. They are more interested in the look of the product, or in how the product will enhance and improve their position and situation. These people need to feel that they have negotiated the best possible deal every time. Guarantees and after sales service are taken for granted, they simply expect it all, yet pushing your after sales services and guarantees, (if you have definite and provable ones) can often get you the sale.

Demanders may not be all that thorough or interested in looking at details. Often they are focused on the bigger picture. It's likely they are less sensitive to others and they do not see the need for being too friendly with a salesperson. These customers may look or sound flashy and they like to show off. Chances are they talk fast, talk big, and use colourful language. They see themselves reflected in their possessions and in others around them.

One of my first big sales the day after I opened my first store in Elizabeth St. Melbourne, was to one of Australia's richest men, back in 1970. I advertised some products, he came in, said he liked the attitude of my advert and stated what he wanted to buy. I panicked. He wore an overall painted with various blotches of dirt and coloured paint, on his feet a pair of thongs, his hair needed combing and his glasses were half broken. Fortunately, I managed to overlook all that and eventually made the biggest sale of my first year in business. This man was a demander, a captain of his industry and he bought 10 cameras and 100 rolls of film asking merely for me to recommend what I thought was best.

Phew, that was it. He wanted neither details nor justification just the facts and 'fast game was a good game' (as my grandmother used to say).

Demanders might fear the detail of too much work, so if you ask them to do an awful lot of extra work or study they may find that off putting. Still, they work hard toward their goals, within their own needs and scope. They love enthusiasm and praise and like to be seen as winners. If they are very much into their demanding attitude they may well think in terms of 'get them first or they'll get you.' Price can be a big concern –they want to win every game and salespeople usually make this worse by concentrating on the price issues. Putting trust in people they buy from does not come easily; the salesperson has to earn their trust. Demanders are more likely to be risk takers and usually make decisions quicker, even hastily.

If these people find you boring, slow, or offering too much, or the wrong information about features etc, you won't get the sale. *You need to be enthusiastic, ask them a lot of questions about themselves and show a lot of interest in what they do.* Though they like to be admired and praised, they are not stupid; in fact they are rather clever as a rule (never assume that anyone is stupid).

As usual, watch for buying signals. Demanders take less time to arrive at a decision. Ask for the sale in no uncertain terms. Directness may work well, but pushy, as usual, will not. Include the customer as always in the close of the sale, by making them feel that they have made a good decision. It is good to ask questions like 'Have you settled on this one?' or 'You seem to like this model' or 'You made the right choice.' Importantly these clients are likely to buy extra accessories so "Will you take the extra accessory pack with it?" or "I think you can see that for your purposes the tripod is a must?" are good approaches.

Moving Away – Defector customers

The away-defector type does not want over friendly communication, or anything that even vaguely sounds like a personal question. Your product focused questions will be reasonably answered and a reasonable product will be purchased. No razzmatazz necessary. Details and features may or may not convince them. Be efficient, not overly enthusiastic, not pushy, but not non-caring either. These people are often extra suspicious of salespeople. Usually they are more interested in results and in supporting documentation so no drama eventuates later.

Defectors are unlikely to take much risk, but might be prepared to do some extra work. However, they won't want increased involvement. These people will tell you as little as possible about themselves or about what they really want or would like. Often they will listen quietly and intensely, watching to see how genuine you are. Because they offer little feedback you may need to prompt them frequently, but do not come across as forceful; that will send them running.

These people as customers can be detail and result oriented; sometimes this is hard to find out. Usually they have done some homework and have a good idea of exactly what they want, especially because they feel that others cannot be trusted. But again, they may not tell you what they know up front. These customers are less responsive, perhaps shy types who are not into long chats, not even when dealing with non-personal issues like buying a product. They tend to see themselves as thoughtful or alternatively they may display a 'don't really care' attitude. If you lose them they never come back. If you get their business they are likely to stick with you. Their way of keeping their own power is to keep their own counsel, not letting anyone come too close. In business, they may be great at technical details rather than at creative output.

You need to follow their rhythm and way of dealing carefully. Do not be afraid of asking for the sale, but time it right. You can ask directly, something like, "Will it be cash or credit card?" or indirectly, depending on how your presentation has gone, or in any way, but you will have to ask for the sale. Recall that commitment does not come easy to defectors so you may have to help them make a decision. Do this as you would with any customer, by reassuring them.

'Result and detail' orientations.

In addition to our three main personality groupings there are a couple of other orientations attached to customer personalities. The 'result' and 'detail' orientations maybe attached to any of our three basic positions – Deferrers, Demanders or Defectors.

RESULT ORIENTATION

These customers want great results from a product in order to show off their ability and/or to profit from the results. A lot of industrial or commercial buyers fall into this category because they are buying a machine or product to help them make more, cheaper, or better products. This is subtle, as we are saying that they are less interested in the actual product than they are in the result (benefit) that the product will produce for them. Thus, whether the product is big or small, the latest or otherwise may not be the benefit point to make. *Everyone wants good results and* benefits, but to this customer you better prove what great results will be *achieved in very efficient and obvious ways*. For example, a comparison of actual results will work better than just saying that one item is better than the other.

The result-oriented customer tends to be a bit (or a lot) of a perfectionist. In a way they need to be. But they can also see if a product presents risks in respect to getting an outstanding result. So, if they doubt they are going to get the best results, then they won't risk buying the product. It is more likely for this type of persona to be a 'demander' and entirely focused on the results. Some of the signposts for this orientation are: efficiency is a must at any cost, likes others to appreciate their efforts, not afraid of hard work to get top results, hates to waste time and effort. They tend to be thorough and efficient, probably less sensitive to others, and they may be happy to justify the means by what they see as good outcomes. They demand to know facts more than usual, but each feature has to point to the possibility of a great outcome (the benefit they want!) They will take well thought out risks, providing the risk factors are balanced against the possibility of good outcomes.

When dealing with these customers couch the benefits of what you sell in strong, provable terms with facts and examples. Be efficient and keep reiterating the potentially good outcome of your product and company. Don't talk vaguely about facts, take care not to be too friendly or excited, and be wary of using humour, unless they do.

THE DETAIL ORIENTATION

These customers tend to hail a bit more from either the deferrer or the defector solutions, but not exclusively so. They are usually over invested in the product's features more than in the results. The benefit for these people can be the great new technology, or the wonderful feature details of a product. They will be impressed with amazing technical details and expect you to know them well. If you come across a bit fuzzy you'll lose them. Often, they have done a lot of research on your merchandise before they talk to you. Serve them very efficiently. Find out what they want in detail. What else since they are fact and feature detail oriented? This client will be more interested in what you actually know about the product. Recall what we said about selling benefits. Every time you talk about a feature you must attach the benefit the feature or detail brings.

CHAPTER 8

EXPLORING HUMAN BEHAVIOUR, CONDUCT AND PERFORMANCE IS EXCITING, BUT IT CAN BE CONFUSING

Some people may find that there are confusing aspects in this whole exploration of self and others, so I suggest that you begin by looking at your own communication style and personality type. Do that without discussing it with anyone at this stage. Also, it is helpful to do your initial self-exploring on paper or on your computer, briefly and spontaneously.

First, write a list and include *whatever features you think you have, both good and bad*. On another list write what 'pushes your buttons' how you feel or react to the things you react to, at work or in private life. Try to use only a few words, just enough to indicate the ideas/feelings. Don't justify why you are like you are, or who has done what to whom, just state what and 'how' not the 'why.' By focusing on your own style many of you will find new feelings and features of your own, leading to new or improved abilities that will become useful to you.

I emphasize that you need to understand your communication styles and types, your 'solution' first. Recognize which solution groups you belong to, at least as far as selling goes. You cannot understand others better until you understand yourself. In my experience most people manage to do this quickly and easily enough. You can reconsider you 'solutions' later, but make a start now on knowing yourself, at least as far as selling is concerned. Until you have a clear point of reference on how you operate and what your strong and weak points are, you will not be able to access those parts of yourself that will work best for you. What to change or leave un-changed in your style is the question.

Once you've understood your communicating style and your personality type, it is time to check your perceptions about yourself with others. Ask other people how they see you and compare how you think you are with the way you are seen. Try a variety of people, including family, friends and work colleagues. You will need to (briefly) explain to the person what you are doing and that you are asking for feedback. Assure them that it is safe for them to give you honest feedback. There is no need for them to justify why they see you in a certain way. Keep the feedback short and clear. No argumentative deep and meaningful talks are necessary, so do not get engaged, just listen and say thanks. What you hear maybe correct or otherwise, that is something only you can decide, but if several people think that you come across in one way, and it's different to what you think about yourself then take a deep breath and consider it!

At this stage I still suggest you make some brief notes. After a look at the feedback, put it away and forget it for a week. Then look at it again, considering it a bit deeper. Don't argue with the way you are seen; what others see is you after all, it is the way they see you. Do this exercise with at least four or five people; perhaps two at work, one at home and a couple of friends.

The feedback you get is the way you are perceived by others. Can they be wrong? Yes off course. Suppose you think that they are incorrect in the way they see you? Ah, this calls for you to ask yourself why that is so. You need to question the 'style' you use to project yourself out there and why it is seen differently to what you intend. *Be on your guard, particularly if you don't like what you hear.*

Most of us easily discard other's opinions if we do not like what we hear. Don't do that for there is something very worthy in feedback. *Keep in mind that no one can win them all, yet recognize that people who are more flexible and less dogmatic can hear feedback better than those who hold onto their own opinions too tightly.* So if you feel yourself reacting to feedback, tightening up, this is a sign that tells you something about yourself. Beware and be aware of what you tell yourself.

Should you then go and work hellishly hard to change some of your personality traits and communication methods and styles? Yes and No. First, recognize and accept *how and what you do* at the moment. Note that I used 'do' rather than 'what you are.' It is a wonderful thing to know that *what you 'do' is not all you are; far from it. It is easier to change what you do than how you are.* That is why I said that it is possible to effectively *change your communication style*. On the other hand I am not saying you can, or should change anything and everything, just because you want to. We have limitations, but we also have potential flexibility once we are more familiar with our communicating style.

Now you are ready for the second step, and that is to look at someone you know (and trust) and see where you think he/she fits the types and styles, the solutions, according to our scheme. Once you have decided what personality type and communication style they use, simply have a chat with them. Explain what you are doing and why briefly. All you will do here is to check out your perception of them, with them, and see if that differs with how they perceive themselves. To begin with, explain simply and quickly the three basic positions. Do the same with several friends or family members and evaluate the results. Then, start applying it at work. Caution: do not go to work the day after you have read this, half baked, inflicting it on the business you are in.

Another good piece of research is to check this scheme next time you deal with any salesperson. Those sellers who are least in touch with their own personality are the ones who come across as most unpleasant, unbelievable and untrustworthy.

Move into all this slowly, but not at a snail's pace. Take a few weeks to look seriously at yourself, your type and style. Take another two weeks to get feedback on how others see you. Allow four weeks to ponder on what you have learned and observe all this in your own, and other's daily actions. This is an initial learning stage. The work of exploration never stops. It is up to you how far you wish to go.

Sometimes a look at your personality and communication style will tell you that you might be in the wrong profession. If this is true for you then stop wasting your life selling – do something else. An awful lot of people simply do not have the right personality type or style to be in the selling business. But, everyone can improve their communicating styles without changing their basic personality.

There is sensational learning to be gained from all of the above, not only for your working life, but also personally. Such explorations of yourself result in you getting more comfortable with yourself and equally importantly, others becoming more comfortable with you.

You know how people often speak of 'personality clashes.'

Sounds simple, but what exactly are clashes? A 'clash' is simply that your communication style does not gel sufficiently with another person. A clash is something where each of you has reacted to the style of another. Fewer clashes, more agreement and better deals at work and at home will result if you care to work on it. In business you do not need the same amount of 'gelling' as you do when you want to communicate with a partner, the children, mum or your mates. You know how you seem to just get on with some people and yet everyone has had experiences when buying or selling, when there was an instant so called personality clash. This is an interesting concept. To 'gel' is to be in close and sticky contact. To clash is to fight and/or to move away.

At this point I need to repeat that it is neither possible nor a good idea to try to 'box' people into a set of rules, of anyone's making. That cannot be done anyway since people are infinitely and subtly varied. It is dangerous to try to over simplify human life, the most complex thing we (do not?) know. Hopefully though, you might agree by now that some understanding of personality types and of the various styles of communicating attached to them will offer a powerful tool when selling and communicating. That is all we need. Great leaders can use this sort of understanding to wonderful effect at times, and unfortunately, with dreadful outcomes at other times. The people who understand others well and use their understanding of the way people behave range from the lowest monsters to well-intentioned saints. From political tyrants, to good men like Nelson Mandela, they all have a better than average understanding of human nature and how it can be influenced.

We are looking for adaptation and flexibility not manipulation.

What I am offering and suggesting for you to do is not manipulation, but 'adaptability' – a productive concept. The thing is that you can keep to the truth and be flexible and adaptable in your communication style. Being customer focused, committed to honesty and to professional relating in life brings better results. Some people say that to sell is to manipulate. Yes and no.

A psychiatrist friend has read the chapters on personality types and styles and handed it back to me looking somewhat ponderous. I asked what the problem was. He liked the ideas, he said. Particularly, he liked the idea of being able to quickly form some sort of framework around personality types and communication styles. And being a shrink, he was happy about my suggestions about self-exploration in order to improve business and personal lives. He knew about the original authors of those ideas and uses them in his profession. However, he was uncomfortable about the manipulative nature of selling, what he termed as 'manipulating' people by knowing how to 'push their buttons' – as he put it.

We debated the matter at length. *My position is that we all manipulate each other knowingly or otherwise to some degree.*

> Rather than to manipulate, I think we are entitled to influence each other in a productive and positive sense.

I figure it is better to know what I am doing than to be ad hoc, to be living accidentally. I argued that understanding more about how we deal with one another will bring not just better results for both buyer and seller, but also a nicer, smoother and kinder piece of communication. If you pay attention to how others operate, what they need, what they like or dislike, then all you are guilty of is trying to make things smoother and more satisfying for both of you.

THE 'DANCE' OF RELATIONSHIPS; HOW THE DIFFERENT SOLUTIONS MIGHT CLASH OR GET ON WITH ONE ANOTHER

Imagine the potential 'dance' of relationships. Like at a dance you respond to a move from another who reacts, and on it goes. That is how it ought to be, but like my example about dancing, we often find that we are dancing alone; you doing your thing and me doing mine. It has to be better than this when we are selling and relating. *Relationships are what we are talking about right through this book whether we are selling a product or looking for and dealing with a partner for life.*

Clearly, intimate relating is at a different level to selling, but picture and ponder on the following: how would two 'demanders' get on in a marriage or partnership? It will be exciting for a while and then arguments and much drama and noise will eventuate. They'll get stuck into each other because each needs the same: much admiration that demands that the other partner gives in. Neither can readily do that as they are demanders whose primary orientation leans toward getting rather than giving.

Oh, so you think that a demander might go well with a deferrer? Sounds good at first. Many marriages I think, do work like this initially. Eventually, the deferrer gets tired and resentful of continuously giving, and yet rarely getting all they need which is constant assurance and love. The demander pushes for their partner to get bigger and better as a person, and gets 'on with it.' If the deferrer moves in that direction, the demander feels less important, less in charge and does not like the change. The demander really wants someone who continually looks up to them uncritically; a deferrer. There is a conflict in both parties, a conflict that is not easily solved by either partner.

All right then, how about a nice quiet peaceful liaison between two deferrers each wanting to give and get love. Now surely this sounds good? This too can work for a while, forever perhaps. It isn't going to be all that exciting when two people are too careful to challenge each other. When both defer to the other neither actually gets as much as they need. Both may be short changed emotionally. There is what appears to be peace and quiet, usually ending in resentment, or boredom. If either party breaks out of deferring even momentarily, the other will be shocked, hurt and lost.

What about a defector married to another defector? There will be little drama here and even less personal growth or satisfaction. Boredom and loneliness will be covered up; the two will live together like friends sharing a house.

Why am I telling you about all these personal relationship problems in a book about selling and doing business?

At a different level all the above applies not just to partners, family and friends, but also to the boss, other workers and most importantly to the way you relate to your customer. The personal examples sound dramatic, but let's transplant some of the last few propositions to selling. Here we do not need a long term commitment, in truth it is 'fast game is a good game' (grandma again…) Actually, when you are selling, it all happens so fast that if you miss doing it right you have missed the opportunity.

Consider a dogmatic and negative 'demander' seller serving a customer who is a 'deferrer.' Can you see what is likely to happen? If you are a salesperson coming from a real 'demander' position and you are not aware of it, and your customer is a 'deferrer' and you do not see that, you will lose the sale and never know why.

The demanders, with their usual enthusiastic and perhaps slightly arrogant manner, will not suit the 'deferrer' customer unless the seller is very careful. For example, a demander will push for the sale and there is nothing more off putting to the deferrer than being pushed. The two styles do not fit – think about all the traits we hung on them. The demander salesperson needs to use their positive powers asking questions, the right ones, from a deferrer customer who will like that approach as it shows interest in what they want. Let's consider the opposite.

What happens when a salesperson who is a deferrer is trying to sell to a demander?

A salesman of mine with many years of experience was a lovely bloke, knowledgeable and friendly, and a bit of a deferrer. He made good enough sales, but he used to bore the hell out of the excitement seeking demander types. Many of these customers love buying big; several were managers buying large parcels of products. You could tell that these demander customers could hardly wait to move on when facing my 'nice' salesman. If, for example, they pushed the salesman for a better deal he'd be hurt and tried to offer silly explanations about the price and about how well he had tried to advise them. The salesman seemed to feel that the customers owed him a sale for his patient and informative services. Eventually the pushy customer would nail him to a yes or no about a better deal, and the salesman would then lose heart and the sale was often lost. Remember, it's likely that deferrers, be they customers or salespeople, may turn on you if pushed too far.

The list of examples and problems could go on and on. Think about how the variations would affect each other. *It is always up to the seller to adapt their style to suit the customer, not the other way around.* This is so important that I shall repeat it: It is

SELLING IS NOT *JUST* TELLING

always up to the *seller to adapt their style to suit the customer, not the other way around.*

CHAPTER 9

BODY LANGUAGE AND TIME MANAGEMENT

I have included only the very basic ideas on body language and time management. However, the following points are important. Body language and time management are of utmost importance to everyone in and out of business.

BODY LANGUAGE

People react to what they see both consciously and unconsciously. There is a great deal to this subject, perhaps some of it has been over stated. Be aware of what your body language says to other people, for whether you realize it or not, it is certainly saying a great deal. You need to be familiar with your body language in order to be good at selling and relating at any level. Often, people do not get on because their words appear to clash with their body language. Customers note body language even more than the words they hear. Here are some of the key things to understand when considering body language:

- Eye Contact

- Use of hands and gestures
- Facial expressions
- Posture
- Movement type, style and direction
- Speech rate and tone
- Spatial distance to customer
- Personal appearance.

Experts on body language state that on first meeting our impressions of others are made up somewhat as follows: 7% verbal, 38% message and tone of voice, 55% visual – that is your body language. First impressions are mainly taken from the messages portrayed by body language (55%). What body language expresses is extremely important right through the sale. It is either helpful to the communication and the outcome or harmful. It's never neutral. The 55% visual however, is not about your pretty face or the red jumper you are wearing. Body language is not about good looks or fashionable clothes. We all know people of unremarkable looks who are somehow attractive and other 'beautiful' people who are not. What clothes you wear need to be appropriate not expensive or show off. Some people have a sense of style that may help the visual presentation, but it does not hide actual body language. For example, you have seen salespeople who greet customers while leaning back against the counter, or are not face to face. No matter how good their words of greeting, these people are 'leaning away' from the customer and the message to the customer is that they are not really interested in serving. Great communicators always 'lean' toward the person they are speaking to and that conveys the attitude, 'I want to be in this conversation.' When I say lean, I do not mean an unnatural body stance; you don't want to look like the leaning tower of Pisa. Not facing your client, fiddling with things while you speak, being too close or too far from the customer, all send the wrong message.

Your tone of voice is thought to be the second most important factor. *Overall 93% of what you present to the customer is made up of the visual body language and the message contents and tone of voice you use. Your message and tone of voice will be more appropriate when your body position is conveying interest.*

What you can do about body language?

- Learn something about your body language by observing it, and by observing other people and how theirs affect how you feel toward them. Get feedback from others about your body language, tone of voice and the words and expressions you often use. When watching a movie, study the actor's body language and how they use their body to portray the characteristics and drama of the scene. Read a book on the subject.

Changing your body language is not 'acting.' It is simply becoming aware of what you project and then actively changing or adapting as best you can.

Time Management

Alan Laker wrote a terrific book on time management called "The Time Of Your Life; Your Life Is Your Time." He said that it is not the time in your life that matters so much as the life you put into the time you have. According to Laker, time is a curious commodity:

- Everybody has the same amount of time each day
- No one ever feels they have enough
- You cannot save time, store it, manipulate it or accumulate it
- You cannot make up for it, what's gone yesterday is yesterday's
- Time is irreplaceable
- Demand does not make time dearer or cheaper
- Time is priceless, and will run out
- One thing is for certain; you have all the time you have.

Time is not the problem, how you use it, what you do with it, plan it, may be a problem. Think about this; your time is your life.

Learn to manage your time. Reasonable time management results in improved productivity, better relationships, less stress and more profit for you. What actually happens when your time seems to just slip away? You feel overwhelmed by all you have to do. Something is wrong if this is how you feel.

The fact is that most of us waste and spend a lot of time on things that we could give up, throw out, or at least reduce. Lots of people take far too much time on things that matter little. Students spend a lot of time binding their books rather than studying. Office people shuffle paper constantly rather than take action on them. Salespeople talk too much concentrating on issues they should disregard, and many business people spend lots of time on minor issues they could delegate to others.

A lot of 'no time' problems are actually personality type or communication style problems. If you think that your job is overwhelming your life, then something is very wrong about your time management and about your priorities. Your job must not entirely drive all your life. Work and what we put into it is important, but not at the total expense of living sanely and well in a good time/life balance. There is a famous saying, *"Will what you do so you may do what you will."* Meaning that either you decide and plan or else you will be dragged along by time and life. Either you take charge of your time or your life will run frantically from one crisis to another.

Here are few simple rules to consider helping you work more efficiently and with less stress:

- *Handle what you can just once. Do it now. If you picked it up, take some action on it.*

- Prioritize, let go of less important issues, delegate, do not procrastinate.

- Include enjoying your life in the management of your time.

- *Stay flexible; don't make plans you cannot change if necessary.*

- Do not make a time consuming job out of time management.

- Have a daily, weekly, monthly 'to do' book, not bits of papers and notes.

- Read a book on time management. It could save your lifetime.

If you think you have no time to think about this, you are thinking very badly.

CHAPTER 10

CREATIVITY AT WORK AND AT HOME

One of the great problems of our time is stress and boredom at work. Repetition of nearly any sort of work is likely to bring boredom and stress resulting in a lessening of productive activity. If we get bored, we lose enthusiasm always leading to stress in various forms. Boredom, stress and depressed moods rise together and they can come from the same basic source. In many professions repetition is all but unavoidable. In the selling profession it is avoidable if you care to work at it.

Those not in the selling profession may think that selling should never get boring because salespeople are always meeting new customers and offering new and various products. This ought to be true. Yet most customers do meet a lot of bored and boring salespeople who seem uninterested in what customers are saying. These salespeople repeat parrot fashion, pretty much what they always say and do. No wonder they get bored, lose enthusiasm and even get depressed.

SELLING IS NOT *JUST* TELLING

What happened to the people who feel that their jobs are not all they hoped for? Many young salespeople started out with great promise and hope, ability and talent. I believe few selling organizations pay sufficient attention to loss of enthusiasm. If an organization sees such phenomena, (and it does take some intention to do so) they usually have pep talks or bring in a 'motivator' or they send their people to sales training programs. This is certainly a step in the right direction, if these motivators and trainers are up to the job. However, companies frequently pay a lot of money for sales and motivational training that many of their salespeople do not want to go to, and the company gets very little real results. Some trainers do no more than repeat what they have always done or are also bored. Or else they pay little attention to the individuals and individual selling situation they are now addressing. One might wonder if trainers have fallen into the same traps as those they are supposed to train, when they offer the same selling scheme they have always offered to every profession and product area.

I suspect that what is missing here is three fold. Firstly, you simply cannot train people without great insight into what they do and what problems they face in their particular industry. Secondly, the training template must be altered to the individuals in any group, in creative ways. Otherwise a lot of training dollars are wasted and account for why so many salespeople do not like going to training sessions.

Thirdly, and very importantly, is that no matter how well people are trained there has to be on-going activity to reinforce training. The workplace needs to be organized in such a way that it challenges the people it employs to stay creative. Loss of creativity results in loss of interest, unless we are very careful and take active steps to keep recreating and re-inventing what we do. In some measure, this is the responsibility of the company, but it is also the responsibility of every salesperson.

> You like to buy from great salespeople who are not jaded or boring because they have retained their enthusiasm for their profession.

Why do we lose creativity? How come some people are full of creativity while others are not? What does creativity mean in real terms, in terms that may help our daily life and work? Everyone is creative in certain areas of their life. A person bored at work may be a creative gardener. A good teacher will create new learning processes for students. Parents need to be very creative with their children or go crazy. Successful business people often pursue other interests and hobbies in which they can be differently creative. We tend to be more creative pursuing our hobbies, **more playful**, and more inclined to try new things.

When we come up with a creative idea it feels good. Yes, then there is fun in it, fun and excitement in trying the idea and some satisfaction, even if it does not work out brilliantly. Saying that what each of us has to do at work or at home is repetitious and does not lend itself to creativity could dismiss a lot of what is proposed here. But hey, this is not good enough and leads us nowhere. Blaming it on society, our job, or our situation may be partly true, but if that is what you think then that's even more reason to work at it.

Creative selling and living is kind of playful.

Bohm and Peat, in their book Science, Order, and Creativity, state that creative activity is not to be regarded as a problem solving exercise, but rather an activity to be 'played' almost for the play itself. In creative thinking/playing, nothing is taken for granted and everything may be put up for re-evaluation. The idea of 'what if?' thinking will be familiar to many people.

I caution that 'what if' thinking may put the brakes on the creative process because it asks, too early, for presumed outcomes. I am not suggesting that it is possible to think of doing something without at the same time thinking of the presumed outcomes. Usually one thinks along these lines: 'If I do this, will A or B happen?' The actual outcomes of new ideas put into practice cannot really be known until they are tested. Thinking up ideas is easier than doing the work of putting those new ideas into practice. It takes commitment and courage to try something new.

Playing with ideas, words and concepts does not necessarily bring about fresh perceptions or brilliant ideas. However, without it, it seems to be very difficult to break through the same old pre-set patterns. In fact, it is probably everyone's experience that nothing stops creativity faster than when we actually set out to be creative on our own. If we brainstorm an idea with several other people in a bouncy and free manner we have a better chance of a solution. Sometimes it is enough just to define and consider aspects of the problem and then perhaps later on, often when we least expect it, we find some great new ways of doing things.

For creativity to flow within us there is the need for us to be receptive, open and active. In order to be receptive we need to be open not just to input from other people, but particularly to our own ideas and feelings. We need to switch off the 'critic' within for a while. This need not be a very heavy activity though it is a serious piece of intentional work.

The first question to ask is how does our creativity work when we are communicating with ourselves? It is easier to change our own receptivity, idea and moods etc. than another person's. The truth is that most of the time we cannot change another person. All we can do is to make changes for and within ourselves, and take action. This might facilitate changes in others around us.

We are inclined to fool ourselves to a degree. We sell ourselves good and bad, useful and useless ideas. The words, illusion, delusion and collusion all have the Latin root of: ludere, which curiously enough actually means 'to play.' Illusion implies playing false with perception, delusion implies playing false with thoughts and ideas, and collusion is just playing false with others and the situation around us. Individuals and businesses sometimes tend to come up with things to support their own illusion, delusion, and collusion. Seems to be the human condition to do so, but it is a lazy and painful one. Then again, we are all very creative in an illusory and delusive manner in rationalizing feelings and situations in order to not have to change things. We are real champions when it comes to playing false to ourselves.

This is where our emotions and self-communicating style comes in. Self talk, our own thoughts and feelings have to be carefully observed or they may work against us. Things go very wrong if we pay scant attention to what we are telling and therefore 'selling' to ourselves. We do not tell all to another, we certainly tell ourselves a lot more, but usually a touch massaged around. A little rationalized, a bit deluded perhaps.

Creative living and working.

There is an old Jewish story, which tells about how one day God answered the prayers of a very wise man, a rabbi.

The rabbi died and found himself at heaven's door facing an angel. The angel told him that since he had been such a good man in his life he could ask any question he wanted.

The rabbi wanted to know whether there was a heaven and a hell and what the difference was between them. The angel smiled sweetly (they always do) and assured the rabbi that there certainly was a heaven and a hell and that there was a big difference between the two places. But the difference was not always obvious unless you were very wise. Then the angel said, "Fly this way (no walking up there) and I will show you hell first."

They came to a big, beautifully decorated hall full to the brim with men and women. The roof was open and the sun shone mildly warm. There was sweet music playing and many angels bringing in the most delicious foods and drinks one could imagine. But as the rabbi looked he saw that they were all very thin, unhappy people silently sitting at the tables laden with all that heavenly food and drink. All the people looked and obviously were very sad and hungry.

It was very quiet there, depressing, no one was talking to anybody. The food on the table was sensational. Many different delicacies were beautifully served steamed on the table. "How come they are not eating?" the rabbi asked. The angel answered the rabbi's question.

"You see that each person has a spoon and a fork but the spoons and forks are so much longer than their arms that they cannot put the

food into their mouths. So there they sit throughout eternity," sighed the angel. *"hungry, unable to eat, forever titillated by the best foods the heavenly cooks could produce. This, dear rabbi, is hell."*

"Oh lord, this is terrible," the rabbi muttered, feeling much compassion and the beginning of some hunger. The angel nodded in agreement. They flew out of the room and the angel said, *"Now we go next door to heaven where you will see, oh wise rabbi, how close hell is to heaven."* They landed right next to a room marked 'heaven.'

Here the room looked surprisingly, even obviously the same. Sweet music filled the air; angels flew about delivering exotic foods to already laden tables. However, the noise in there was deafening! Everyone was talking and laughing. Everybody looked well, even better than when they were alive, the rabbi noted. The rabbi's guiding angel had to yell above the happy sounds of contentment asking if the rabbi could see the difference. The rabbi looked and looked.

"Hm," he muttered, "it looks the same but different." And he stroked his beard. Rabbis are very wise and always have beards. He looked again. The room was just as beautiful, the tables and chairs, the music and the food seemed the same as in hell but why were these people so happy and how come they were eating? The rabbi noted that everyone was eating and yet everyone had the same long, long spoons and forks as those next door in hell; utensils longer than their arms. "You see the difference?" asked the angel again.

"No, I can't," muttered the bewildered rabbi. "Everything looks the same."

"Yes, oh wise one," answered the angel. "Everything is the same with one exception. The only difference is that here the people have figured out that they can feed each other with the long spoons and forks."

The resolution, the great outcome one sees is often obvious only after it is found. The solution to the problems of hell was creative, simple and elegant. Everyone had to communicate and co-operate. No one was left out. The team found the right solution. Everyone received a benefit. The difference between hell and heaven is often a thin line...so to speak.

Creative thinking is the scientific model.

The scientific model rather simplified is as follows: You have certain current perceptions and expertise. A new idea about how to do things better is put forward and is followed by a conceptualization, enabling you to propose something new that might be acted upon. Once the idea is tried it is then examined as to its outcomes, relevance and implications. The very important step is to go into action and then to evaluate the results or outcomes in several ways:

- Were there any results at all?

CREATIVITY AT WORK AND AT HOME

- Were the results satisfactory?

- Were the results not good enough, but heading in the right direction?

- Were the results negative and if so, what does this suggest?

The whole set-up is then re-explored as to how and why the outcomes were negative or positive. The process may then be repeated with appropriate changes.

Many years ago I was talking with Robo, who was then the general manager of Ted's Camera Stores. We were bored with the tired old line 'Can I help you?' and trying to replace it with something more interesting. We thought that the customers must also be bored with it. (Struth, I hate the 'how are you today?' starter.) A few days later Robo told me that he had a great new line with which to greet customers: "Have you found what you are looking for?" It sounded all right to me so we went downstairs to try it out in the store. Robo walked up to the next customer and popped the question. The customer looked surprised and said, "Huh, beg your pardon?" In other words, the customer was surprised at not being asked the old 'Can I help you' question. Robo's line had gained the customer's attention.

Three footnotes to that story: We had tremendous trouble trying to get salespeople to adopt the idea for a new starting line; some of them just could not do it. What was achieved, however, was that most of them agreed that the old 'can I help you' was boring and they looked for new lines too. The idea stimulated creativity and enthusiasm. For a while that seemed to fire them up to a degree. Just the fact that salespeople talked to each other trying out new ways of approaching the customers was fun and broke the routine. The problem was that though many tried new ways of greeting customers they soon lapsed back into the old forms. The experiment was thus, partly successful as several staff members developed new ways of approaching customers.

Any new or creative idea, which cannot be acted upon, is not likely to be a good idea. Not for you and not in the present set of circumstances. Whether a creative idea is actionable or not is a reasonable indicator as to whether it is a productive idea or whether it just seems like one. If it is too complex, too expensive, has too many opponents and so on, then the idea may be a pie in the sky. However, even failed ideas may bring changes that improve the original problems and situations.

When we 'action' a new idea we bring together familiar expertise with new ways and thoughts. If we did not use old experiences, know-how and perceptions, we could not possibly be thinking of a new and creative version of whatever it is that we set out to do. But watch it carefully because often what we bring in is as old as the hills, re-inventing the wheel with an extra spoke. Nonetheless, if it is new to us in this current situation, that may be fine.

∼

I have already proposed that if you do not have the basics of selling at the level of 'automatic competence' then any good idea about selling may turn into a potential mess or nothing much at all. If you do not have the basic skills and information then creative ideas will end up being a pie in the sky. That is perhaps why many people come up with what sound like great ideas, but never action them. You know how at a football game there are eighty thousand people who 'know' what the footy star should be doing. Ha ha. At a restaurant we all know how they could speed up service or cook better food. Ha, ha. I have some terrific ideas about many things I know little about. Ha, ha again, though it is possible, if rare, for this to work out.

> Any new idea or behaviour that is turned into automatic competence will free the mind to be yet more creative.

The knowledge or ideas, that are automatic do not take up a great deal of energy or time once they are embedded.

Nothing stays the same forever. Most people will agree that nothing stays the same but it is a curios human trait that we tend to go on repeating the same old things anyway. It is easy and comfortable to do that.

We cannot take any of our knowledge-assumptions as being correct forever without constant further questioning. The world around us changes technically, biologically, and physically. Our circumstances, situations, desires, needs, wants, goals and aims also change. Perhaps this is why we sometimes surprise ourselves about our values and belief systems as well. We hold those usually as unassailable and yet at some point they might change in us, as if by themselves. In reality, what has changed is that other aspects of our lives have moved on. The assumptions held often from long ago, are simply no longer valid or applicable. Everything changes constantly. All that we can rely on is the idea of flux and the need to watch and act, within our world. Creativity is never static, or finished, not something you do once. On the contrary, it is ever changing and change-able and that is precisely why it can never be boring.

Intentionality, Commitment, Awareness leads to Creative Action.

We have to assume, accept and rely on many things in life. We think of doing something, we consider our actions, we take or leave certain actions and then we evaluate the results. We do this knowingly. There is nothing unusual in that. *Make this a more aware, more intentional process.* That means doing the process with consciousness, commitment and purpose.

Do not let living a non-creative, boring life bite your ankles. Fight back. Get moving and the movement will take you further. Once on the move it is easier to keep going. It is one of the laws of physics; the law of motion and inertia shows that it takes more energy to start things moving than to keep them moving.

Managers, Leaders, Action

Creative action often involves others in your organization. Professor Ellyard in his book, *Ideas for the New Millennium,* makes the point very clearly about the difference between managers and leaders. What he says also shows the difference between ordinary and creative thought.

> Dr Ellyard said, "Managers respond to change while leaders create change. Managers are concerned about **doing the thing right**; leaders are also concerned about **doing the right thing.** Managers work in the organization while leaders work on the organization."

Doing something truly new needs both leadership and good management. The old saying 'No guts no glory' has a lot of truth to it. Leaders create; managers implement and follow what is created. One measure of whether a new way of doing things is actually new is that the fresh action usually involves some hard decisions and initially some extra effort. There will be many obstacles. There is resistance within us and often a lot of resistance from those affected. I don't know from where I heard this next most important idea, but I see it happening all the time:

CREATIVITY AT WORK AND AT HOME

People do more and more of what has never worked.

People do more and more of what has never worked.

People do more and more of what has never worked.

If that is the case, then we tend to do less and less creative thinking and action. Creativity won't happen just because we like the idea of being creative. What stops us from activating fresh innovative ideas even when we really like them? We have unconscious defence mechanisms working against new ideas that appear to threaten our current balance, routine, mindset, value systems and beliefs. Anything that challenges our pre-recorded programs is likely to be answered by the entrenched and dogmatic emotional decisions we tend to be stuck with. We often hold onto outdated modes of thinking and acting as if they were fundamentally important. Some few may be but many, if not most, are not important anymore. Sometimes these are the very things that hold us back. If we could ease up, open up a little, then we may be more open to change and to new or different points of view.

I reiterate: to respond or to change situations the ideal action is a mix of current knowledge and past experience, via the filter of the creative attitude. This rarely happens for most of us. When it does, we know with certainty that a truly creative solution has happened. 'A breath of fresh air' a new way of doing things and finding a better way makes us feel excitement and satisfaction which speaks its own truth.

CHAPTER 11

SELF-ACCEPTANCE EQUALS SUCCESS?

What is the idea of self-acceptance doing in a book on selling? Just this – earlier we touched upon the idea that you may have talents and abilities that you know well and other capacities, flairs, gifts and abilities you barely even suspect.

What is the 'self' you are asked to accept if you do not know all of it? Accepting one's self is a strange paradoxical idea popularly sold to us as a good thing. It would be a splendid thing indeed, but first you need to be very familiar with yourself. The popular suggestion is that you are the way you are, and that ought to be accepted as it is. But first the question is how exactly are you? Do you know what you have, how you are and how you present to others? There are parts of you so hidden that they can actually act against you without your knowledge. Some things in that computer you call your brain box are capable of bringing satisfaction, success and more meaning into your life; other aspects of your mind might be working against you.

My thinking is that you can improve certain aspects of your life while accepting what and how you are for this minute or day or week or year. Until you accept what there is for now, it is indeed hard to move on to greater things. Curious as this seems, consider how it works; to accept how you are requires you to understand how you really are now, how you operate, relate, think and feel. You need a certain amount of self-awareness and knowledge. To become more aware of all your hidden talents you need to explore yourself honestly and steadily. The more you know about yourself, the more you will know and understand about others, leading to more sensible and successful choices in your life. Some people are compelled to do this without prompting, while most of the population are afraid to explore themselves at all. They say they don't need it, that it's all nonsense etc. etc. Most people either do not know that they are afraid of looking within deeper, or they deny it. But why be afraid? You won't find anything awful deep in there, I assure you. What you will find usually is extra depth, talents and abilities. Yes, you might also find some needs and wants denied and unknown, and these may feel a little uncomfortable, but the process of looking at yourself is a freeing one in itself.

Great personal power comes through self-knowledge.

That power has limitations dependent on many factors. The idea is not to spend your life wishing and dreaming about what may have been, or blame others, your parents or society (though of course they have had a great influence on you), but to actively see what you can now do and achieve that will offer you satisfaction and meaning at work or at home.

Life is a process. It is a way of travelling rather than arriving at a final destination.

Life is not so mysterious; it is just a continuum of how and what we do. I doubt that people with lots of money are on the whole any

SELF-ACCEPTANCE EQUALS SUCCESS?

happier than those with much less. I'm certainly not suggesting that the poor are as comfortable as they could be if they had more financial security and safety. People have various opportunities, backgrounds, good or not so good parenting. Some people are open enough to take up the challenge of making the best of what they have, others less so. Not all of this, I confess, can be controlled. But we all have a certain ability to change and explore ourselves no matter whether we find it easy or not to do so.

The challenge and meaning of life is neither to give up, nor to accept your lot as it is now.

Accept what you need to for now, explore and change what you can. Have a go with intent and commitment at bringing more into your life, that is all anyone can ask.

SUMMARY

MAKE MORE SALES, STOP SELLING. FIND SOLUTIONS AND INFLUENCE OTHERS.

Selling, as a whole, needs re-framing. In my approach, I wanted to differentiate and emphasize the following aspects:

- You must know the selling steps by heart, which means you will need to have 'automatic competence.' Selling is not just telling. It is focused communications.

- You need to understand why each step works, not just how it works.

- *There are many parts or features to your personality.* Find and use the ones best suited to whatever job and communicating you are doing. Living with increased awareness of how you really feel and what you really think will make both your job and personal life more satisfying.

SELLING IS NOT *JUST* TELLING

> If you are aware of your responses and choices you are in charge of your responses.

Make an effort to see everyone and each situation as unique. It is not so much what work you do, but how well you do it that matters. We can all do anything we are doing a bit better. However, be wary of reaching for too much, be realistically ambitious not a dreamer. Have a purpose, aim and goal in life. In other words, do what you can and accept what you have done. In this way you can then, after all say, 'This is what I chose to do.' Choose what you want and strive for it carefully; many things seem desirable, but some turn out to be not so great.

Creative thinking about life and your work is a must and it is a continuing affair. Without creative thought and action, work and indeed life becomes boring and does not pay you well in any sense. The more you understand about your motivations, the more you understand about other people. Personal awareness is the most important thing for any human being. With it, you can sail the calm and stormy waters of your life far better. Without it, you are a rudderless ship without power. Take responsibility for your life, whether you want or like what has happened to you so far or not. You have some choices, you can do better that is for certain, but you are not in full and absolute control either. There is a famous old Jewish saying:

> *"Plan as if you were going to live forever, live like today is your last day."*

Accept what there is for now, and enjoy life. Do the best you can to improve your life at work and at home. Be kind to yourself and to all there is.

I wish you Happy, Sane and Successful Solution Selling.

Ted Todd

MAKE MORE SALES...

Ted's other books: Non Fiction - self-help- for thinkers:

'The Software of the Personality' which discusses how to find the best version of yourself in life.

Fiction/novels:

'A Doubtful Inheritance'

The story weaves through time and places, from 1945 to present day from Budapest to Argentina, Melbourne, Los Angeles...There is a huge inheritance to be had if...But what else do we inherit? What are the sad and happy memories we have 'inherited' that make and fill our lives...The two main characters chase not just the money but a lot more. (This work was part of the creative component for Ted's PhD work)

'Fifty Something Male is Looking for a Woman...'

These are fictional stories; about the adventures and mistakes, the joys and the sadness of men who are looking for a new intimate relationship after a long term marriage. The stories show what men do, think and feel, how they approach attractive women and what goes wrong, or right. Alternately serious, deep, funny, and with much pathos and insight, Ted writes from the heart and mind of the male.

www.ingramcontent.com/pod-product-compliance
Lightning Source LLC
Chambersburg PA
CBHW071912290426
44110CB00013B/1360